The Rational Project Manager

A THINKING TEAM'S GUIDE TO GETTING WORK DONE

Andrew Longman

Jim Mullins

KEPNER-TREGOE, INC.

WILEY

John Wiley & Sons, Inc.

Published by John Wiley & Sons, Inc., Hoboken, New Jersey.
Published simultaneously in Canada.

For general information on our other products and services, or technical support, please contact
our Customer Care Department within the United States at 800-762-2974, outside the United
States at 317-572-3993 or fax 317-572-4002.

Wiley also publishes its books in a variety of electronic formats. Some content that appears in
print may not be available in electronic books. For more information about Wiley products, visit
our web site at www.wiley.com.

Library of Congress Cataloging-in-Publication Data:

Longman, Andrew, 1959–
  The rational project manager : a thinking team's guide to getting work
done / Andrew Longman, James Mullins.
    p. cm.
  ISBN 0-471-72146-8 (cloth)
  1. Project management. I. Mullins, James, 1973– II. Title.
HD69.P75.L66 2005
658.4′04—dc22

                                              2004027083

Foreword

Back in 1965, when *The Rational Manager* was published, times may have been less turbulent, but they were no less challenging: Competitive pressures were beginning to intensify, as the Japanese and European economies rebounded from the aftermath of World War II; boom-and-bust economic cycles continued to challenge forecasters; the "Age of Acquisitions" had begun, with high-stakes financiers stalking the trail, looking for low-hanging fruit; the Cold War continued to cast its chill; Vietnam, the Kennedy and King assassinations, and the LSDing of America created confusion and cynicism; racial tensions were boiling; and bestsellers such as Ralph Nader's *Unsafe at Any Speed* and Rachael Carson's *Silent Spring* caused great anxiety throughout corporate America.

Into this swirl of events, Charles Kepner and I inserted a new type of organizational player: the *rational manager*. We used this term to describe someone who was not only adept at problem solving and decision making, but who was also *consciously* competent.

In other words, the rational manager understood the critical-thinking *processes* behind problem solving, decision making, and planning, and this understanding opened up the possibility that such processes could be imparted to others. Problem solving and decision making were no longer a matter of the genetic endowment of a gifted few; everyone's skills in these areas could be significantly improved. Most importantly, by transferring critical thinking skills in problem solving and decision making to a broader group of managers and workers, organizations discovered that they could achieve far higher levels of performance and superior results.

And they did, which is why Kepner-Tregoe has enjoyed continuous success since its founding in 1958. Not only did American companies such as General Electric Company, General Motors Corp., Hewlett-Packard Company, IBM, Sun Microsystems, Inc., and hundreds of others put rational-process approaches to good use—so did companies around the world: Fuji Film Co. Ltd. and Honda Motor Co. Ltd. in Japan; Telekom Malaysia Berhad in Malaysia; Keppel Corp. Ltd. in Singapore; BHP Billiton, Boral Ltd., and Visy Industries in Australia; BAA PLC, GlaxoSmithKline PLC, and Vodafone Group PLC in the U.K.; Porsche AG, Siemens AG, and ThyssenKrupp AG in Germany; Compagnie de Saint-Gobain, Thomson SA, and TOTAL SA in France; and on and on.

Much has happened since the appearance of *The Rational Manager*. One of the great shifts in organizational life that has occurred in the past 45 years has been the globalization of the modern business enterprise. It has made getting work done exciting, challenging, and often very frustrating. Today's project team leaders, at least the truly effective ones, are more akin to orchestra leaders than generals. They command top performance within a diverse setting without *commanding*. In such a context, the rational processes for managing projects and getting work done discussed in *The Rational Project Manager* become an important tool for delivering projects on time, on budget, and on business objectives, especially within organizations challenged by cultural diversity, geographical distances, time zones, and reporting relationships.

A second great shift involves the teaming of the work environment. Teams—and the projects that occupy them—have become the way work gets done in the modern enterprise. While individual talent and accomplishment will always be valued, the high-performance superteam has come to replace superman as the enduring symbol and source for organizational success.

Books have a way of following need, especially in the business category. And, while bookshelves these days are littered with a vast number of books on project management, few, if any, provide guidance on the critical thinking that is essential for project success. Andrew Longman and Jim Mullins, two colleagues of mine at Kepner-Tregoe, have moved beyond the individual rational manager to his and her twenty-firstt-century counterpart: the team-focused rational project manager. Their book not only offers readers the tools, techniques, and tips for effective project management, but it presents a comprehensive discussion of the problem-solving and decision-making processes that are pivotal to effective project management and execution.

Project teams don't operate in a vacuum. They function within a larger performance system. Andrew Longman's and Jim Mullin's book makes an invaluable contribution to the art and discipline of project management by linking behavior within teams to five key performance variables. These variables form the basis of all performance systems, and when they are aligned with team goals and behavior they transform project teams into a powerful force for producing results.

Since *The Rational Manager* and its numerous subsequent editions have appeared, Kepner-Tregoe authors have written many books, on subjects ranging from strategy to organizational well-being to productivity improvement. One common denominator of everything we have written is our bias against abstract theorizing. We prefer pragmatic discussions aimed at producing ideas for action. *The Rational Project Manager* follows in this tradition, and its unique format enables readers to drill down to just the right level of detail to facilitate understanding and on-the-job application.

Like our other books, *The Rational Project Manager* was written close to the action. Its concepts and approaches have been hammered out on the anvil of client experience. During the past 20 years, more than 150,000 people around the world have learned the Kepner-Tregoe project management process and have applied it to projects large and small, ranging from product development and launch to construction to maintenance to information technology to strategy implementation.

Put the book's lessons to work in your organization, and you will undoubtedly harness the thinking power of teams at every level of your organization. You will make every member of a project team able—and determined—to succeed.

Benjamin B. Tregoe
Founder, Kepner-Tregoe, Inc.

Acknowledgments

Plain and simple, this book could not have been written without the pioneering work of Jim Schlick. As Kepner-Tregoe's head of Product Development in the mid-1980s, Jim surveyed the project management landscape and saw it littered with tools and methods: network diagrams, critical paths, Gantt charts, resource allocation, earned value analysis. What was missing, Jim found, was a simple, systematic, rational approach to defining, planning, and implementing projects.

Jim researched the best project management tools, charted the thinking processes behind successful projects, and assembled the results into a rational methodology. This process approach continues to be a distinction and strength today, as Jim Schlick still consults for Kepner-Tregoe as a partner and project management expert. He has served as a mentor to the authors in their professional endeavors, and his ideas form the core of the book.

The book also relied on sound editing, proofing, formatting, and project management expertise from many others. Specific thanks go out to Matt Holt of John Wiley, for embracing this book from the outset, Christabel Nazareth for her keen literary eye and objective critique, Dale Corey, who persevered through several drafts, and Judie Morello and Irene Worek, who prepared the manuscript for consideration. We would also like to acknowledge Ben Tregoe, who introduced us to a conscious approach of clear thinking and effective action; Dan Lochmann of DaimlerChrylser, formerly of Kepner-Tregoe, who helped to shape the method closer to what it is today; and the hundreds of clients and learners who, while we were helping them, taught us something about how project work really gets done.

And where would we be without our literary agent, friend, and mentor? Peter Tobia of Market Access is the force behind the publication of *The Rational Project Manager,* and we thank him sincerely.

Andrew Longman would also like to thank: my parents, who taught me at a young age the benefit of planning and organization during our many family camping trips; my wife, Chrysanthe, herself a mother and master project manager and source of support and inspiration; and my brother Phillip, the author, for the role model and advice he provided.

Jim Mullins adds his thanks to Jen and Kira, for loving me despite my demand for obsessive planning; my mom, who taught me the value of extreme dedication through her work with special needs children; and my brother and sister, Mike and Colleen, for always being there for me, no matter what.

About the Authors

Andrew Longman is a partner in Kepner-Tregoe, Inc. He is also director of marketing and product development, responsible for the design, development, and delivery of Kepner-Tregoe's service products as well as the worldwide promotion of the company's brand and consultants.

Mr. Longman helped design and implement eThink®, Kepner-Tregoe's critical-thinking support software, and its project management software, Project Logic®. He has also been instrumental in the design of a Web-based version of Kepner-Tregoe's Problem Solving and Decision Making®.

His clients include American Honda, DRS, Kimberly-Clark, Lockheed-Martin, Daimler-Chrysler, Procter & Gamble, and TRW.

With a bachelor of science in psychology and philosophy from Northern Michigan University, Mr. Longman is certified by the Project Management Institute as a project management professional (PMP).

Jim Mullins is Kepner-Tregoe, Inc.'s worldwide product manager for eThink®, a software system that supports the use of problem-solving and decision-making skills to resolve project issues and capture lessons learned.

Mr. Mullins consults with Pfizer, Masterfoods USA, GAF Corp., Interbake Foods, Brunswick Corporation, and many other clients in a variety of industries, analyzing and structuring clients' performance systems to improve project results, transferring critical-thinking skills, and installing project management. His work with clients has led to their solution of numerous high-priority issues, resulting in savings of millions of dollars.

Holding a bachelor of arts degree from the College of the Holy Cross, Mr. Mullins is a member of the Phi Beta Kappa honor society.

Contents

chapter
1

the missing pieces
of the project
management puzzle

PICTURE THE MEMBERS OF a project team exchanging comments during the lunch break of a recent management course. They are fuming over their latest debacle: a project to select and tee up a location to produce hi-tech vehicle components for a major partner. After eight months of scouting the available workforce, persuading home-office employees to relocate, estimating labor costs, submitting proposals to the local zoning board, and detailed planning for the construction and start-up of the new site, the project was abruptly terminated. Here's why: A senior manager at the partner organization suddenly decided, for reasons unknown to the project team, that the location just wouldn't do.

PROJECT MANAGEMENT AS THE NEW IMPERATIVE

Why wasn't the senior manager involved in the selection process from the beginning? What other work didn't get done while the organization devoted significant resources to the project? And what was the true cost of the eight months of wasted work?

The costs of such failed projects are tremendous, and they fall into two categories. The first—direct costs such as wasted materials, overtime, additional manpower, and the continual revision of plans—are relatively easy to calculate. Take the case of "The Big Dig," a Boston, Massachusetts, public works project aimed at improving the driving conditions in one of America's most congested major cities by dramatically overhauling its roadways and tunnels. The project has been going on for 17 years and involves politicians, contractors, designers, engineers, and residents. In a 2003 article, the *Boston Globe* documented $2 billion in overrun costs by the company responsible for the project.[1]

Boston is not alone. In a watershed study of 7,000 IT projects initiated by U.S. corporations and government agencies in 1998, the Standish Group found that 88 percent are behind schedule, over budget, or both. *The direct cost of these project failures is over $145 billion each year!*[2]

The second category, which goes beyond the direct costs, includes indirect costs, such as missed opportunities, sullied reputations, and the loss of competitive advantage and employee and customer goodwill. Consider the much ballyhooed Constitution Center in downtown Philadelphia. The tourist attraction opened its doors on the weekend of July 4, 2003, with a ceremony that included political and civic dignitaries. In the middle of the proceedings, a large steel plank collapsed onto the stage, sending Mayor John Street to the hospital and nearly hitting a supreme court justice. Philadelphia became front-page news, but for the wrong reasons. Although it's impossible to calculate the number of tourists who have stayed away as a result of the mishap, the loss for the city of Philadelphia has been very real.

Failed projects engender fear. Organizations that miss the mark time and again lose their willingness to take risks and commit to new endeavors, no matter how attractive the project or how obviously it is needed. This "projectitis" can lead to lost opportunities and risk

[1] Eileen McNamara, "The Big Dig and Blame Games," *Boston Globe*, December 17, 2003.

[2] Jimmie West, "Show Me the Value," *Training*, September 1, 2003.

aversion, the costs of which can never be calculated (but are surely significant).

Then there's morale. Employee satisfaction is closely tied to feelings of accomplishment. Dragging a project out indefinitely or killing it in midstream is a real demotivator. Members of the project team begin to leave or transfer, decimating the organization's talent base and likely increasing the organization's toxicity level, as former team members spread the word far and wide. And the first to exit are often the organization's high performers—the ones who gave their all, contributed a high degree of expertise and skills, took risks, and were frustrated once too often.

So the costs for failed projects are significant. But what about organizations that execute consistently? Successful organizations use projects to create value . . . and turn that value into customer satisfaction and bottom-line results. To succeed in an increasingly complex business environment, they must consistently complete work on time, within budget, and, most importantly, achieve their project goals. As the major platform for value creation in today's organizations, projects are too important to be left to chance. Each must be managed, from start to finish, using a consistent, sound, agreed-upon process.

PROJECT MANAGEMENT UNPLUGGED

Project management, in today's business environment, usually entails the use of multiple calendars, complex schedules, financial data, PERT and Gantt charts, and various reporting systems. A review of the project management literature reveals the existence of a wide variety of techniques and approaches to planning and executing a project. Competing software packages abound, although 75 percent of the organizations that use project management software say that Microsoft Project® is their software package of choice.[3]

The existence of all these tools and techniques has created a de facto working definition for the term *project management:* the use of a set of tools and techniques to manage a combination of money, time,

[3] James J. Jiang, Gary Klein, and T. Selwyn Ellis, "A Measure of Software Development Risk," *Project Management Journal*, September 2002.

people, and work. Given this definition, many organizations base their project management approach on the notion that, with money, time, and people, work will get done effectively. But this definition misses the mark. Many of today's popular project management tools and techniques were created years ago by military engineers seeking a tighter grip on the time and cost of accomplishing work, as well as how to best report their findings in a meaningful way. These can be hugely valuable tools, but project management is far more than just documenting work, costs, and adherence to schedules.

True, software and paper-based tools that track the expenditure of resources and time are often integral to the communication and documentation of important project data. And money and time are essential pieces in the project management puzzle. However, there are more important processes and ideas that lie at the heart of a complete definition of project management.

Project management comes down to getting people to do "stuff"— hopefully "valuable stuff"—and to do that stuff in an effective, timely manner. The stuff is a one-time series of interrelated tasks that must be completed within a budget, by a specific time, to achieve desired results or meet a specified need: moving corporate headquarters, upgrading a telecommunications infrastructure, implementing a corporate strategy, reengineering a business process, launching a new product, investigating and correcting a deviation. These are all examples of projects. They represent change that will be defined, planned, implemented, and, most importantly, managed.

PROJECT MANAGEMENT IN ACTION

Think about superior watches, luxury clothing, and elaborate lighters. Now think about selling these products to high-end consumers around the globe and maintaining, if not improving, a reputation for precision and class.

It's not your typical project management story. But, one year, preparing for the annual industry trade show in Geneva, Switzerland, became a top priority for a luxury producer of men's fashion and accessories. The company's leadership had decided that trade-show sales should constitute the lion's share of overall sales in watches, lighters, and cufflinks. For the first few years, substantial company resources, from people to money, had been devoted to the preparation for and operation of the show. Sales had been solid during that time, but every year shipping delays, unavailable stock items, and other last-minute problems left those in charge with persistent concerns.

Granted, preparing for the show was a complex project, especially when shipping, customs procedures, and trade regulations for both the display goods and those that would be sold on site were considered. In addition, measuring success against goals like "improved reputation" and "competitive advantage" was difficult. But management felt that the show should run more smoothly and attain even loftier goals with respect to sales and company image.

Wisely, before sinking additional resources into the project, management took a step back and looked closely at the problems they had encountered in past years. Their conclusion: The overall approach to planning for the show had always lacked direction and consistency. Individual managers had approached their pieces of the project with different tools and techniques. Depending on which function they represented, members of the planning group had differing ideas about what success should look like. Scarce resources and competing priorities had made it difficult for the planners to remain focused on goals. Even more worrisome, the investigation of past trade shows revealed that it wasn't just that things seemed out of sync at times: Sales had actually been lost due to the chaos.

Preparing for the show was a complex minuet that involved a number of departments—marketing, product development, logistics, hospitality, and sales—over an eight-month period of preparation. This led management to make two key changes in planning for the next show.

First, they swallowed hard and made one person responsible for the overall management of the project, which in previous years had been managed by an ad hoc committee. As a dedicated resource, the new project manager had time to approach the project more rationally. She was temporarily relieved of all other responsibilities, freeing her up to develop a set of project management practices that could be put to use immediately. For example, with input from leadership, she created a project statement, a set of objectives, and a project plan that included over 375 separate tasks. At this point, her team was poised to begin its work in a well-ordered, sequential fashion.

The second change involved project communication. The project objectives and plan served as the basis for all meetings and decisions. As a result, meetings were no longer a rehash of what everyone already knew. Instead, they were held to resolve predefined concerns with the project, make modifications to the plan, and list next steps.

By making these key changes, the company went back to the fundamentals and, more importantly, defined and planned the project before any work began. Morale rose, as project-team members appreciated the more buttoned-up approach. Few last-minute problems surfaced. And the new approach brought tangible results: Average meeting time was slashed from three hours to 45 minutes; six weeks were cut from the overall time required to prepare for the show; the $655,000 budget was met; and sales spiked by 50 percent.

THE STUFF OF PROJECTS

Project management isn't a new phenomenon. Human beings were getting "stuff" done as far back as the beginnings of America. Think back to the days when Native Americans were hunting buffalo. Or even farther back, to the building of pyramids in ancient Egypt. Although it didn't carry an official term, a one-time series of interrelated tasks was at the core of the work accomplished by each of these groups.

Picture a group of Native Americans preparing for a buffalo hunt, which at first glance may not appear to fit the definition of a project. Using a method known as the *piskin*, large piles of rocks, tree stumps, and buffalo dung formed two converging walls, each over a mile in length. The open end was a grazing area; the closed end narrowed to a low hill, with spears around the fence. The piskin construction and hunt were monitored by a leader; there was a set goal (a dead buffalo); there were required resources for building the temporary walls; there was a set time (the tribe could only go so long without food); and there was a carefully thought-out plan of work, with each person having an assigned role and responsibility (like the "caller," who wore a buffalo robe and lured the buffalo into the trap). A piskin usually resulted in a kill, and, in this regard, it was not just a project, but a successfully managed one.

The Egyptian pyramids are an even more visible example. To this day, the structures continue to draw scholars and tourists to study the engineering marvel and disciplined work that produced them. One of the most compelling aspects of the pyramids is the management required to complete them. Designs for the final structure, even when constructed on a grand scale, were extremely accurate. Enormous numbers of human resources volunteered—or were volunteered—to toil on the project. And feeding the mass of humanity was a project in and of itself. Workers received three meals a day, delivered on time. An angry and hungry workforce was a major detriment to project success.

The Native Americans and the ancient Egyptians carried out their "stuff" in an organized, timely way. They accomplished their work using the most basic management practices. And they accomplished their goals, time and time again.

TODAY'S PROJECTS: WHAT MAKES THEM DIFFERENT?

Today's organizations sport an arsenal of tools and high-powered software, and project management—as a term and a practice—has never generated as much insight and interest as it does right now. (A recent Google search turned up over two million hits for the term *project management*.) There is even an organization dedicated to gathering and disseminating an official body of project management knowledge: The Project Management Institute. Membership has grown over 22 percent in the past year alone, and the PMI claims nearly 84,302 certified, active project management professionals (PMPs).[4]

Why all the commotion over the current project management environment? As we've pointed out, organizations exist to accomplish

[4] "PMI Fact File: Statistics Through June 2004," *PMI Today*, September 2004.

work—work that will deliver value and achieve the goals of the organization. Most of today's work gets done in projects and on project teams. (An estimated 10 trillion dollars a year is spent on projects around the globe.) Completing this work in the designated amount of time, within a budget, and with desired results has never been more important; it's the price of admission for today's lean, dynamic organization. Yet, the nature of work has become dramatically more challenging than when it consisted of killing buffalo and building pyramids. Today's projects are far more varied and complex, and they require a far more sophisticated system of project management.

Think about it: How do you manage a project when it will be planned by one function and implemented by another? When it's entirely new work, requiring new capabilities? When a customer wants a different result this time? When competition demands rapid innovation? No question, today's organizations must be more dynamic, dialectical—and, some may say, diabolical—when it comes to managing projects.

TODAY'S GAME IS SPEED

Fast forward to the modern project and consider the case of a large consumer products company that discovered how to produce a mature product with an exceptional new twist. Not only was the product itself "invented," but so was the equipment needed to produce the new feature. The work was extremely complex, and the launch deadline called for the project to be completed in half the usual time. What's more, the company knew that a fierce rival planned a similar product launch for the following year. The opportunity to capture coveted market share was now or never.

Under pressure to carve out a unique competitive advantage, today's companies must scamper for new ideas and services; embark on technological upgrades; attack quality issues with a vengeance; and redesign their strategy, business processes, policies, procedures, and responsibilities to support the economy's new demands. And, as never before, managers are being asked to complete these jobs in geographically scattered, highly networked organizations, with outsourced and/or shrinking resources—all while aiming at ever-loftier goals.

What's left is a matrixed structure of intertwined functional groups, departments, and people who are asked to navigate the complexity to accomplish the work, and to accomplish the work in the form of projects.

DISEMBODIED GOALS

Today's typical goals—implementing a new strategy or completing competitor research, for example—are not nearly as easy to define as they were in the old days. A dead buffalo and a monumental pyramid are tangible, visible targets that people can see, touch, and smell. A partially implemented strategy, on the other hand, does not stand out quite as much as a half-completed pyramid.

Take the case of a long-time manufacturer of home goods. As the 1990s came to an end, the company realized that, like many other American businesses, it had slowly moved away from production as a competitive advantage. By 2003, the company's leaders recognized and consciously decided to focus on what could become a true strength: brand image and customer satisfaction. But there was a flaw in the plan: Using its existing production methods, the company was unable to meet its newly ratcheted-up delivery and quality goals. To succeed in its new strategy, a major shift in manufacturing methods would be required. The company took a deep breath and began a massive project to overhaul its antiquated systems.

But the expected outcome of the project was murky and, in truth, never fully communicated to the company's employees. At the end of the fiscal year, which turned out to have been a tough one, the project was officially shelved for an undetermined length of time. Some parts of the project had been completed; others had been left unfinished. The company limped along with some effort focused on new goals and some dedicated to running operations the old way. They had invested millions of direct and indirect dollars but never were sure what success would look like—or if it was worth the sacrifice.

THE EBB AND FLOW OF TODAY'S TEAMS

Even if the final outcome is clear in a modern project, the people tapped to contribute to it aren't quite the same as they were in early America or ancient Egypt. The people and skills needed to complete a pyramid were as well defined as the goal itself: engineers to design the structure, an artist to paint the structure or carve some designs, a carpenter to cut the wood, "strong backs" to do the lifting of stones weighing up to 15 tons, and someone to orchestrate the various types of work.

Some modern projects have clearly defined goals, and, therefore, the skills needed to achieve those goals are relatively easy to identify. But, more often than not, today's projects have less tangible end results and, therefore, require more complex skills. Creating 10,000 lines of high-quality usable software code or a redesigned delivery process requires a skill set that may not be easily identifiable and includes such intangibles as creativity, analytic ability, and critical-thinking skills.

In addition, many members of today's project teams come to the task with a set of technical skills but are uncertain as to how those skills will add value to the overall project. As a result, it can be difficult for them to readily appreciate business objectives or customer perspectives. This makes it tough for them to come together as a team and apply their expertise appropriately.

To further complicate matters, project workers often split their time between not just one, but several, projects and their "regular" job. In the case of the home-goods manufacturer turned marketer that we discussed earlier, people were pulled into the project from almost every department and functional group in the company. They were expected to meet the daily demands of their regular job while taking on the additional work generated by the project, and the extent and priority of their contributions were never clearly delineated, nor were the personal consequences to individual team members considered.

THE COMPETITION FOR RESOURCES

Today's project managers must deal with the fact that few, if any, of their resources are under their managerial control. And chances are that more than one project or business manager is competing for the resources that are needed to successfully complete a particular project. Even when a resource has been assigned to a project manager—for example, one project manager has been promised 25 percent of a programmer's time—it doesn't mean that priorities won't change and promises won't be broken. What's more, what does 25 percent really mean? Two hours a day, every day? The same two hours each day or whenever the programmer has some spare time? One day a week? Every Monday or a different day each week? Whatever the arrangement, it may cause the project to be understaffed at critical times.

THE REVOLVING DOOR

With so much reliance on knowledge and unique roles, many of today's projects are jeopardized when an expert member of the project team departs. In the mid-1990s, organizations lost people because of the booming economy: Knowledge workers became free agents, signing on for the biggest chunk of cash or the most "fun" workplace. Then, after the economic slowdown of 2000, organizations downsized and restructured at a breathtaking pace. Both scenarios made it clear that losing people or moving people into new jobs is a reality, no matter what the economic conditions. Project managers often deal with new people or newly transferred people throughout the life of a project. The notion of an intact work team, reporting to one leader for the entire life of the project, is wishful thinking. There needs to be a method for crisply and effectively bringing people into and out of projects.

THE PENCHANT FOR COMPLEXITY

Today's projects are both a cause of, and a response to, the complexity and do-more-with-less anthem of the modern business enterprise. Starting a new project may be a good or bad decision for an organization. Regardless, it adds to the fabric of complexity because it pulls resources from other projects and activities, crosses departmental and functional boundaries to ask strangers to work together to achieve a goal, and doesn't always start with a clear sense of direction and priority. Even projects aimed at reducing complexity swallow people and budgets and often require inter- and intradepartmental communication.

Today's business enterprise presents a host of challenges for project managers that were never even dreamed of before: people scattered around the globe who hold critical knowledge and skills for completing tasks; people moving in and out of the organization; increased reliance on contractors and vendors; business groups that tend to adhere in a group rather than cohere as a project team; too much work being attempted at once, by too few people. Consider one public utility's conundrum. At one point, the mid-U.S. utility had 140 projects underway—with a staff of only 125 employees to complete the work!

PROJECTS AREN'T GOING AWAY

Despite the drawbacks, projects remain the pivot point for organizational change. And, if carried out effectively, projects remain the best method for cutting through the complexity to accomplish work. That's why most organizations consider themselves to be project-based: 50 percent use consultants for project management and over 45 percent have implemented a formal project management office.[5] Which is why most organizations need a better understanding of how much failed projects cost and, more importantly, of what they can do to acquire the missing pieces of the project management puzzle.

THE MISSING PIECES OF THE PROJECT MANAGEMENT PUZZLE

One of the most common mistakes that organizations make is fixing something without fully understanding why it's broken. Taking the time to find out why projects fail to achieve the appropriate results on time and on budget is the first step in improving your organization's project management health.

[5] Norbert Turer, "Tracking the Best Laid Plans—Companies Are Managing Multiple Projects as Diligently as Their Investments and Finding It Pays," *Information Week*, May 19, 2003.

It's easy to dismiss the search for cause with the statement, "Our projects don't finish (insert *on time, on budget, with the desired results* here) because we simply don't have enough people to accomplish the work." Although it may be true that the number of people can't support the number and scope of projects, this is not the *root* problem. Why does your organization take on more projects than it can effectively manage? Is it a conscious decision by top management? Is it the lack of a conscious decision? Is it because company strategy is not clear or not communicated? Is it a failure to execute the strategy rationally?

These high-level concerns are very real and need to be addressed by senior management. The last chapter of this book addresses an organization's inability to place projects in the larger context of the business enterprise. But the lion's share of *The Rational Project Manager* has been written for *you*, the project manager or project contributor. Without strong project management to balance priorities and resources, work will never get done, no matter how strategic it is.

With that in mind, our research—and experience with thousands of projects in hundreds of organizations—suggests that the reasons for project failure fall into three categories:

1. The lack of a common approach to projects that focuses on the fundamentals.

2. Weak thinking about the decisions, problems, potential problems, and complex situations that drive the project.

3. The failure to manage projects within the social context of the organization.

This book focuses on these three fundamental, yet often forgotten, pieces of the project management puzzle: *a world-class, rational process for managing projects; an approach to critical thinking that facilitates the effective resolution of project issues; and a model for encouraging peak performance in people.*

An organization that masters these pieces masters effective project management. But, ultimately, success will be determined by those individuals who stand alone at center stage, responsible for cutting through the chaos and complexity and for weaving the pieces into an improved picture: project managers.

Faced with tough challenges, project managers—and the key contributors tasked to support them—attempt to hit a fast-moving and often unclear target. They need to understand the specific content of the project they're managing and also be a master of project management skills. They must be able to balance politics, personal motivations, and unforeseen problems while motivating a team and striving to meet tight deadlines and budget restrictions. In short, they're a bit like a referee at a sporting event: Do a good job and nobody notices; make a mistake and the finger pointing begins.

Good project managers use the traditional project tools and techniques to reveal important project data. But they understand that the tools are useless without clear thinking to ensure that the data is relevant and meaningful to the project. They arm their project teams—and in some cases, their organizations—with a rational approach to managing all aspects of a project: from defining the needs to constructing the plan to implementing the plan. In the end, project success hinges on the quality of thinking behind the project management tools.

Good project managers are also more than adept at steering the performance of project contributors while negotiating for resources and communicating status and priorities to upper management. And they pay strict attention to the need to resolve issues quickly and effectively: making decisions, preventing problems, solving unknown problems, breaking down complex situations, and promoting opportunities.

In *The Rational Project Manager*, we push aside theoretical exploration, complex formulas, and software-as-savior deliberations. This book outlines the basic, yet largely ignored, rationale of successful project management. You'll learn a logical, step-by-step methodology for managing all phases of a project. You'll enhance your ability to solve people problems and encourage specific performance by using a tried-and-true behavioral system. And, last, you'll be introduced to a set of analyses designed to help resolve project issues, make decisions, and protect your project.

The project management methodology and critical-thinking skills outlined in this book are the cornerstone of getting "stuff" done in a rational, timely manner. And that "stuff" is what allows organizations to remain dynamic, to compete, and to eventually outpace the competition.

WHAT'S AHEAD

The project management process presented in this book is not difficult. It's broken down into three parts: Definition, Planning, and Implementation. You'll explore each part in depth. In fact, you'll receive special *tips* that further explain how to apply the concepts and *pitfalls* that warn you of common mistakes in certain areas of the process.

From time to time, the critical-thinking processes of Situation Appraisal, Decision Making, and Problem Solving will be referenced in conjunction with a step in the project management process. Complete explanations of these rational techniques are included in Chapter 6. You will also learn the principles of influence, involvement, and communication that are so crucial to a project's success. The "Join Together" sections of Chapters 2 through 4 begin to address managing people in projects, and Chapter 5 is dedicated to the topic. And, in "The More You Know" sections, you'll find techniques that may help you manage your project in unique ways.

chapter
2

---

project definition

*M*OVING THE CORPORATE CUSTOMER *Services Department will be a huge undertaking. Although the project manager, Tim Dwight, has seven years of experience in managing complex projects, the rest of the project team is new to the project management game. What's more, many team members hold a personal stake in the outcome of the project; they are members of the Corporate Customer Services Department.*

During the first project team meeting, Tim explains the decision by the company's Executive Committee to move Corporate Customer Services. As the team already knows, an old building houses the current offices, and it's not equipped to meet the department's increased technological needs. In addition, Tim tells the group, the Executive Committee recently agreed to expand the department by adding 45 new people within the next year. The new office provides extra space for the already cramped department and leaves room for the upcoming growth, as well as some additional future expansion. It also allows the company to upgrade the technological capabilities of the department and its work environment. New furniture and décor will be part of the plan.

By the end of the meeting, the group knows that they have three months to plan and conduct the move, and that the budget, provided to them by the Executive Committee, is $170,000. They also understand the need for a smooth, well-managed move and the reasons behind the deadline.

WHY ARE WE DOING THIS PROJECT?

Too often, project teams begin to plan a project before they have taken the time to truly consider why they are doing it, how they are going to do it, and what it's going to take to get it done. There is a tendency to start out by building Gantt charts—project management software prompts this behavior—without considering the fundamental purpose of the project. Jumping to the creation of time lines is often the first, wrong step taken by project teams destined for trouble.

So think about—and then answer—the "why" question before you jump into project planning. If you need some help, consider the following:

- The reasons why the project is necessary for your department, organization, client, community, or yourself.
- The overall purpose of the project.
- The threats, opportunities, and needs that are driving the project.

TIP

Sometimes background information may be provided to you by senior management in a *project charter* or a signed contract. Such a document formally recognizes the existence of the project and gives the project manager the authority to spend resources on project activities. The charter or contract will include the business need for undertaking the project and the results to be delivered. It will also include preliminary product/service descriptions that will have to be refined as the project progresses.

Capture this "why" information as background for the project. You'll use it as you create a project statement and develop objectives, and you may decide to also use it to demonstrate the thinking that occurred prior to the start of the project.

With your background information in hand, you're ready to start the first part of the project management process—Definition. During Definition, you'll answer four basic questions:

1. What is the project statement?
2. What are the project objectives?
3. What needs to be accomplished to complete the project?
4. What resources are needed to complete the project?

This information will provide you and your project team with a framework that will guide the planning and implementation of your project.

Four activities will help you find answers to these questions:

1. State the Project.

2. Develop Objectives.

3. Develop the *Work Breakdown Structure* (WBS).

4. Identify Resource Requirements.

STATE THE PROJECT

Stating the project is the first step in Definition. A *project statement* is a clear, concise phrase that describes the project's overall goal, as well as its time and cost boundaries.

TIP

If you are struggling to come up with time and cost information for your project statement, use ballpark figures until you can get better information. This technique will prompt others to audit your figures and provide you with a better time frame or a more realistic cost.

"Move the Corporate Customer Services Department within three months at a cost not to exceed $170,000" is an example of a project statement. We use this example throughout this book. The project statement contains three elements: (1) An action word with an end result (this is called the *performance* element); (2) a target date for completion (the *time* element); and (3) an overall project cost (the *cost* element). A triangle often serves as a visual representation of these three elements, indicating the need to balance all three.

Take note: The project statement is not merely a group of words; the three elements shouldn't be plucked from the sky, nor should they be a product of one person's or one group's demands. Instead, the project statement should reflect, at a very high level, the reason for doing the project.

TIP

Use the project statement as a communication tool by keeping it visible on all project documentation.

To accurately assess project timing, consider how much time it has taken your organization to complete similar projects in the past. In addition, think about when you'll

PITFALL

Don't be overly influenced by the time and cost of similar projects you've managed in the past. If your current need requires completing the project significantly faster, at less cost, or at a different quality level, then design the work or solution differently from previous projects.

need to complete the project in order to gain or optimize its benefit.

You may be uncertain about including a budget limit in your project statement. However, it makes good sense to do so even at this early stage. By examining cost realistically, you can change the end result—or even the scope—of your project. For example, after estimating how much the project will cost, you may discover that the expected benefit does not justify the cost of the project. If you're struggling to calculate the cost of a project, don't take a wild guess. Instead, wait until later in Definition or Planning (when you'll have factored in the specific cost of resources).

Developing a project statement will focus members of the team on the intended outcome of the project. That ensures that everyone involved has the same understanding of what the project will accomplish, by when, and for how much.

Join Together

When you develop the project statement, involve project team members, key contributors, key stakeholders (including sponsors and functional managers), customers, and experts. Refer to the descriptions of each group:

- *Project team members:* People designated by you or someone else to be on the project team. The project team usually produces the bulk of the project work.

- *Contributors:* People who are not on the project team but who are asked to contribute their time and/or effort to the project.

- *Stakeholders:* People who are impacted by the project now—or will be in the future. Some stakeholders will exert enormous influence on the project, like sponsors who typically provide the political, financial, and logistical support, champion the project, and approve the results; others, like functional managers, provide human and other resources such as equipment, facilities, and so on.

- *Customers:* People for whom the project results are produced; they can be internal or external customers and usually are also considered stakeholders.

- *Experts:* (Also known as subject matter experts or SMEs), these individuals hold special experience, knowledge, or skills that relate to the planning or implementation of the project. They're also considered contributors.

You'll need the commitment and involvement of all of these groups to the project. For example, they may possess critical information that you need to formulate the project statement. Including them in your discussions will increase the probability of winning their commitment and harnessing their knowledge up front . . . and throughout the life of the project.

TIP

Even after you've agreed on a project statement with everyone involved, you may need to revise it during the Definition and Planning stages. Proceed with the revision if it improves the accuracy and relevancy of your project statement.

However, keep in mind that gaining agreement on a project statement may not always be easy, especially if the need for the project (and its value) is not clearly understood among the people involved. If necessary, tap into the list of threats and opportunities that the project will address (you prepared this list prior to Definition), and present it to those involved in project statement discussions. This will demonstrate your thinking, compare it to the thinking and expectations of others, and focus attention on a project statement that best represents what the project should accomplish. Situation Appraisal is a rational and effective method for identifying, clarifying, and prioritizing threats and opportunities. This method is described in more detail on page 176.

The More You Know . . .

It's possible that several different projects could address the same set of needs. If this is the case, develop a project statement for each project. Then, compare the project statements and select the one that will best meet your needs with the least amount of risk and potential adverse consequences. (Keep in mind that you may be forced to go further into the definition and planning of each project to make a fair and accurate comparison. If you invest the time to do this, try combining details of several different projects to create a superior hybrid.) For more information on choosing between alternatives, see page 181 on Decision Analysis.

Before you move to the next activity, take a step back and critically assess your project statement. Are you certain that the project should be undertaken? Are you sure that the project, stated as is, will meet the need or resolve the concern? Confirming that your organization should, in fact, do the project—and that the project will meet the need—is the first step toward a successful project.

DEVELOP OBJECTIVES

At the outset, we recommended that you think about and record the reasons why you're doing this project. Now you'll develop *objectives,* the next activity in Definition. Objectives will further clarify and expand on the reasons for undertaking this project.

TIP

Objectives should communicate the specific value the project will deliver, *not* how the project will be completed.

Project objectives should be written as short statements and should describe (1) specific results and value that the project will deliver and (2) constraints within which the project must be completed.

To develop project objectives that represent *results,* ask the following questions:

1. What do you want to have at the end of the project in terms of benefits or capabilities?

2. What value should the project produce?

3. How will you know when you satisfy each objective? (measure and standard)

4. What short- and long-term benefits do you want?

Your answers will reflect things like: impact on market size, market share or margin; customer satisfaction; quality levels; business and financial results; technological innovations or trends; organizational issues; and facilities and equipment usage. (For a complete list to consider when developing objectives, review box topic 2.1, Helping You Develop Objectives on pages 28–29.)

Example 2.1 on page 30 shows objectives developed for the project statement, "Move the Corporate Customer Services Department within three months at a cost not to exceed $170,000." Objectives 1 through 4 represent results.

Project objectives that represent *constraints* will expand on the boundaries that you set in the project statement and will also consider other restrictions. To write project objectives that represent constraints, ask the following questions:

- What requirements must be met?
- What constraints, restrictions, or resource limitations do we face?
- What resources should be used or saved?

Each project objective should contain a clear measure and standard of performance. Try including the phrase, "as shown by . . ." or "as measured by . . ." at the end of each objective. Then, complete the phrase with information on how you expect to measure the objective and what level of performance you expect, such as a specific number or an agreed-upon value. For example, if your objective is to "Maximize the ability to quickly revise future office layouts," then you can measure the objective by the total number of hours it will take to revise the layout for a workstation and set the standard at "not more than _____ hours per workstation." Or, you can measure the objective by the total cost to revise the layout for a workstation and set the standard at "not more than _____ cost per workstation." Metrics

---

BOX TOPIC 2.1
Helping You Develop Objectives

Project objectives are critical to a successful project outcome because they establish the criteria that you'll use to make decisions about the project and guide the project team.

If you're struggling to compile a complete list of objectives or if you want to brainstorm additional objectives to make sure you have thought of everything, use the following list to stimulate your thinking. For each thought-starter, ask yourself, "How should (thought-starter) influence my choice?"

Thought-Starters for Developing Objectives

HUMAN RESOURCES

Motivation and attitudes
Skills and ability
Performance and productivity
Development and growth
Health and safety
Equal rights and opportunities

FACILITIES AND EQUIPMENT

Space
Flexibility and adaptability
Location
Compatibility

ORGANIZATION

Relationships among units,
     functions, individuals
Discussions
Responsibility and delegation
Formal and informal organization
Coordination
Information systems

MATERIAL

Sources and availability
Quality
Grade
Handling and storage

EXTERNAL INFLUENCES

Economic trends
Competition
Vendors and contractors
Company image, positioning
Law and government
Environment
Community
Technology

OUTPUT

Quality
Quantity
Pace and timing
Distribution

MONEY

Capital or fixed costs and
     expenses
Support, maintenance, and life
     cycle costs
Price
Margin or profit
Return

BOX TOPIC 2.1   Continued

IDEAS AND PROCESS

Security, proprietary position
Knowledge capture and retrieval
Research
Capabilities
Networks

STRATEGY

Competitive advantage
Target market
Product platforms and mix
Market size
Market share
Key strategic indicators

TIME

Life span of project
Life span of output
Time to first return

CUSTOMERS

Marketing
Sales
Support
Location

PERSONAL

Goals and plans
Family
Strengths and weaknesses
Interests
Values and beliefs

like these give the people who have to revise the layout a very precise idea of the scope of the work.

Again, review the project objectives in Example 2.1. Objectives 5 through 13 are constraints.

Most projects will have more objectives dedicated to results than to constraints, but this isn't a universal formula. Some projects will require you to work within very strict boundaries (many constraints), while others will be entirely flexible (few or no constraints).

The primary reason for developing objectives is to provide you and other project participants with a basis for defining the specific work that needs to be done to complete the project. However, project objectives also focus the project team by guiding their decisions and offer other interested stakeholders and customers a summary of the project's intent.

Example 2.1   Project Objectives

Project Statement

Move the Corporate Customer Services Department within three
months at a cost not to exceed $170,000.

Project Objectives

At the end of the project, we will have:

1. Maximized the ability to quickly revise future office layouts.
2. Minimized barriers to information flows (including voice, data, doc-
    ument, and interpersonal communication) among department
    offices.
3. Minimized overall traffic by creating the shortest, most direct traffic
    flows within office space.
4. Provided for current and future storage space.
5. Met corporate requirements for minimum office floor space; light-
    ing levels; heating, ventilation, and air conditioning (HVAC);
    background-noise levels; workspace ergonomics.
6. Not exceeded $100,000 in external costs for moving equipment and
    furnishings.
7. Completed the move within three months.
8. Maximized effective use of existing equipment.
9. Not interrupted current customer requirements and workload.
10. Not exceeded $70,000 for new equipment and office furnishings.
11. Fit office layouts within allocated office area.
12. Brought all computer and telecommunication equipment up to cor-
    porate standards.
13. Complied with government safety and health regulations.

Join Together

The project communication that began around the project statement
should continue while you are developing objectives. Once again,
securing the commitment and experience of your project team members, stakeholders, customers, experts, and key contributors will be
critical to the success of your project. Individuals in each group can
contribute to the development of objectives in several ways—by sur-

facing the original ideas, writing the objectives, refining the objectives, suggesting ways to measure the objectives, or reviewing the entire list of objectives. However, it's critical that you, as the project manager, ensure the list of objectives is reasonable and accurately reflects the value your customers expect to receive from the project.

The More You Know . . .

In some cases, you may find it effective to split project objectives into two different categories. The first category represents primary results and restrictions that will be directly addressed by the project. Designate these under the heading, "At the end of the project we will have . . ." The second category represents indirect benefits and less important restrictions. These can be designated under the heading, "Other project objectives are . . ."

TIP

When developing objectives with large groups of people, using creative techniques such as brainstorming or *Nominal Group Technique* (NGT) will encourage the involvement of everyone in the group. NGT prevents excessive influence by a few individuals by asking everyone to generate ideas anonymously. These ideas are then collected and written on easels or whiteboards. Next, the ideas are clarified in full group and each individual lists the ideas they think have high priority. Finally, the highest-priority ideas are selected from this shortened list.

It's possible that some project objectives absolutely must be met, while others can be satisfied to varying degrees. The absolute requirements are called *Must objectives.* These objectives should be mandatory, have a set limit that must be met, and be realistic to accomplish. Example 2.1 contains a Must objective: Office layouts must fit within allocated office area.

The remaining objectives can be classified as *Want objectives.* Although they may be important to accomplish during the project, they do not have an absolute minimum or maximum threshold that must be met. "Minimized barriers to information flows" in Example 2.1 is a Want objective. For more information on Must and Want objectives, see Decision Analysis on page 181.

Finally, you, your project team, and the customer will use project objectives to assess progress and evaluate performance. After the project has been completed, you'll ask, "How well did we meet each

BOX TOPIC 2.2
The Good, the Bad, and the...

Make sure no objective is repeated or contains more than one requirement and that all your objectives represent "why" you are doing this project rather than "how" you plan to do it. Some characteristics of good and poor objectives that you can use to audit your project objectives are listed below.

Good Objectives Are...	Poor Objectives Are...
Stated in terms of specific end results	Stated in terms of activities, deliverables, features, or processes
Each limited to a single important result	More than one objective in the statement
Clearly stated	Compound, too broad
Achievable in a stated time period	Never fully achievable in a stated time period
Related to the outcome of the project	Ambiguous in defining what is expected
Important to the success of the project	Not of real consequence
Precisely stated in terms of quantities, where possible	Too brief, indefinite, long, or complex
Definite measurement standards and methods	Theoretical, idealistic, or impractical
Formally documented	Verbalized only; assumed to be understood by everyone
A mix of short- and long-term objectives	Either all short- or long-term objectives
Unique	Duplicates or restatements of other objectives

On some occasions, a single objective may mean different things to different people. It's very important to express what you're trying to achieve when you write an objective so that it's clear to you and to others. There's a tendency to want to get away with a minimum number of words. Thus, people may abbreviate objectives into a few terse words and subsequently cause major communication difficulties. It's always worthwhile to ask, "Is (objective) understandable to someone other than myself?" or "What do I/we mean by (objective)?"

objective?" The answers will help you and your customer create a "report card" at the end of the project.

DEVELOP THE WORK BREAKDOWN STRUCTURE

Your project statement and objectives should communicate *what* you're doing and *why* you're doing the project, as well as the boundaries you'll recognize. The next activity, Develop Work Breakdown Structure (WBS), will communicate *how* you'll do it.

A WBS identifies the scope of all the work to be accomplished during the project and organizes it to show how all the pieces fit together. To create a WBS, follow these steps:

TIP

Several major deliverables may support a single project objective, or multiple project objectives may be supported by one major deliverable.

1. *Review the project statement and objectives.* The WBS organizes the work that's necessary to accomplish your project goals. It is the skeleton on which the whole project rests. The quality of the choices made in defining the organization of the work could mean the difference between a successful project implementation and a "death march." So it's important that when developing the WBS, you remember why you are doing the project in the first place.

2. *Create a list of major deliverables that represent the project's overall output.* To identify each major deliverable and accomplishment, ask:

   ▪ What are the major components that must be produced to meet project objectives?

   ▪ What are the major achievements that must be accomplished to meet project objectives?

   ▪ What categories or groupings represent work that should (logically) be managed together?

Your answers to these questions will begin to identify major deliverables that will, in turn, provide the framework for the remainder of the WBS.

3. *Separate each major deliverable into sub-deliverables.* This involves breaking down each major deliverable into its component parts. To help you separate, ask:

- What needs to be done to produce this major deliverable?

- If we were to watch this actually being done, what activities would we witness being completed?

Your answers will become sub-deliverables.

In addition, sometimes it will be useful for you to break down your sub-deliverables into sub-sub-deliverables.

A good rule of thumb: Stop breaking the work down when you've reached the point where primary responsibility can be assigned to one person or one group and a reasonable estimate can be made as to what kind and how many resources you'll need. This is the point where you'll feel comfortable handing the work to someone else, knowing that they'll understand what needs to be done.

The lowest level deliverable is called a *work package*. This is the level at which responsibility is assigned, resources are consumed, and work is completed. (For more information on separating and clarifying, see Situation Appraisal on page 176.)

4. *Select a type of structure for your WBS.* A project structure is a way of organizing major deliverables that will make it easier to manage and communicate. Here are some common types of structures:

- Product-based (major deliverables organized by tangible outputs).

- Process-based (major deliverables organized by workflow).

How Do Your Work Packages Measure Up?

Review your work packages. Do they contain performance standards? Performance standards describe the expectations for the work; ensuring their integration into your work packages will clarify exactly what needs to be done. Performance standards can appear in the following forms:

- *Design specifications*—describe the work package output in terms of physical characteristics. For example, a work package to "dig a house foundation" may state it should be dug exactly five meters deep, 20 meters wide, and 30 meters long.

- *Performance specifications*—operational capabilities the work package must achieve. For example, a work package to "produce a racing engine crankshaft" could state that it must be capable of turning 15,000 revolutions per minute for four hours before failing.

- *Functional specifications*—similar to performance specifications, these describe the required end use. For example, a work package to "produce a computer training room" might say the room must accommodate up to 12 people for training in project management software. It doesn't specify type and quantity of computers, size of room, etc. This gives those responsible for the work package more latitude to find creative, less expensive, and/or better ways to meet the goal of software training for 12 people at a time.

Use the type of performance standard that best reflects the results you want to achieve. It's possible that more than one type of performance standard is needed to describe all aspects of a work package's desired output.

Record performance standards, assumptions you make, and further details about the work in a WBS dictionary. A WBS dictionary is a compilation of the details and history of the project. It will help ensure that work is well understood and can be resourced, planned, and implemented accurately. This will be especially helpful for tasks that are complex, new, or are likely to be handed off during the project. Software packages often allow for the creation of WBS dictionaries.

- Phase-based (major deliverables organized by stages).
- Resource-based (major deliverables organized by type of resource).

TIP

How do you know which work goes together to form a major deliverable? Group the work together according to these criteria—work that will be accomplished during the same time period, share similar resources, be tied to the same output, be funded in the same way, or be done in a particular way because of how the organization is set up.

Sometimes, the project work suggests an approach naturally; other times, you'll need to think about which approach will best help you manage and monitor the project. For example, most research and development project managers choose a phase-based approach for structuring project work. Because future work often depends on the result of current work or research, it makes sense to organize the work in phases like discovery, validation, prototyping, and so on.

At this point, you may consider breaking off a piece of the project and treating it separately as a subproject. For more information on subprojects, see Splitting Projects into Subprojects on page 50.

5. *Record the relationship between major deliverables and work packages.* Each deliverable should be equal to the sum of its work packages. In other words, completion of sub-deliverables should, by definition, complete a major deliverable. Look at major deliverable 1: Office Layouts in Example 2.2. It's broken down into three sub-deliverables (1.1 Relationship charts prepared, 1.2 Department block layouts drawn, and 1.3 Department detailed layouts drawn).

TIP

It may be a good idea to include such work as planning the project, managing the project, conducting project meetings, and closing out the project in your WBS to get a better sense of the total scope of the project.

As a result of completing these three sub-deliverables, Office Layouts is completed. Also notice that deliverable 1.1 is further broken down into two sub-sub-deliverables (1.1.1 Interviews conducted and 1.1.2 Relationship charts drawn).

There are several tools you can choose from to depict this relationship. The two most common are the *indented outline* and the *tree diagram*. Example 2.2 depicts an indented outline. As you can see, the levels of work are indented, and numbering is shown as a 1, 1.1, 1.1.1 system. A tree diagram, on the

Example 2.2   Work Breakdown Structure—Indented Outline

Project Statement

Move the Corporate Customer Services Department within three months at a cost not to exceed $170,000.

Work Breakdown Structure

1. Office Layouts
   - 1.1 Relationship charts prepared
     - 1.1.1 Interviews conducted
     - 1.1.2 Relationship charts drawn
   - 1.2 Department block layouts drawn
   - 1.3 Department detailed layouts drawn
2. Office Equipment
   - 2.1 Equipment to keep identified
   - 2.2 Equipment to order identified
   - 2.3 Office interior designed
   - 2.4 Equipment and office furnishings ordered
   - 2.5 Equipment and office furnishings received
3. Office Area
   - 3.1 Electrical services installed
   - 3.2 Telephone services installed
   - 3.3 Computer services installed
4. Office Move
   - 4.1 Work order submitted
   - 4.2 Equipment and office furnishings moved
   - 4.3 Office furnishings installed
   - 4.4 Equipment installed
   - 4.5 Personal materials moved
5. Organization Manuals
   - 5.1 Customer and vendor notices distributed
   - 5.2 Personnel databases updated
   - 5.3 Telephone directory revised

Example 2.3 Work Breakdown Structure—Tree Diagram

Department Office Move

1. Office Layouts
- 1.1 Relationship charts prepared
  - 1.1.1 Interviews conducted
  - 1.1.2 Relationship charts drawn
- 1.2 Department block layouts drawn
- 1.3 Department detailed layouts drawn

2. Office Equipment
- 2.1 Equipment to keep identified
- 2.2 Equipment to order identified
- 2.3 Office interior designed
- 2.4 Equipment and office furnishings ordered
- 2.5 Equipment and office furnishings received

3. Office Area
- 3.1 Electrical services installed
- 3.2 Telephone services installed
- 3.3 Computer services installed

4. Office Move
- 4.1 Work order submitted
- 4.2 Equipment & furnishings moved
- 4.3 Office furnishings installed
- 4.4 Equipment installed
- 4.5 Personal materials moved

5. Organization Manuals
- 5.1 Customer and vendor notices distributed
- 5.2 Personnel databases updated
- 5.3 Telephone directory revised

other hand, is found in Example 2.3. It shows the relationships between work packages and deliverables using lines and boxes.

6. *Review the WBS.* This activity should not be a mere glance at your outline or diagram. Rather, it should be a close examination to ensure that all project objectives are supported by the work described and all work packages support at least one objective. To review your WBS, ask:

- What objective does this work package support? (If it doesn't support an objective, it doesn't belong in your WBS.)

- Are all of the project objectives sufficiently supported by the work described? (If they are not, this may be an early sign you won't achieve all of your goals.)

- Can all work packages be assigned resources and responsibility? (If not, then the work packages may be poorly worded, frivolous, or in need of further clarification or separation.)

Developing a WBS will help you and the project team determine how you'll accomplish the project objectives. It will also communicate to the project team how much and what kind of work will be expected on the project, and, to some extent, how that work will be managed and controlled. When you have the WBS in place, you and your project team will have the basis for establishing resource requirements, budgeting and pricing, assigning responsibility, sequencing and scheduling, and reporting for project monitoring.

Join Together

Consider involving the same groups of people (project team, stakeholders, experts, customers, key contributors) you included in discussions on project statement and objectives . . . with one exception. If possible, invite current and past project managers who have managed similar projects to help develop or review your WBS. Perhaps more than anyone else involved, they will help you identify omissions, areas for improvement, and potential problems and opportunities.

Keep in mind, however, that you should set expectations about the level and extent of each group's participation. As project manager, you can choose to develop the WBS alone, develop it by involving others in decisions about structure and content, or assemble a group to develop the entire thing. Your choice should be driven by a need for commitment to the project's implementation, as well as availability of information. For more information on managing the involvement of others, see Involving People on page 149.

The More You Know . . .

It's possible that, in your organization, nothing like the project you're going to do has ever been done before. In fact, it's possible that nothing like it has ever been attempted. There are no previous project managers or internal experts to consult, and, consequently, you may find it difficult to anticipate the work required beyond a short time frame. What's more, the structure and type of future work may depend upon the outcome of work in the near term. If this is the case, consider using a technique called *moving window* (also known as *rolling wave*) to plan your project by phases. At agreed-upon time intervals, you and the project team will meet to flesh out the project plan, including more details as necessary to implement and control the next phase of the project.

IDENTIFY RESOURCE REQUIREMENTS

Once you've established what you are going to do (project statement), why you are going to do it (objectives), and how you're going to do it (WBS), you can identify what and how many resources are required to get it done.

Think of the WBS (which you developed in the last activity) as a series of project outputs—a collection of major deliverables that describe what work will be completed. If the WBS is the output, then *resource requirements* are the inputs—things that the project will consume in order to produce the outputs.

The approach to developing project resource requirements consists of identifying three elements for each work package:

1. Type of resources that will be required.

2. Amount of each type that will be needed.

3. Cost of the resources.

Identify which of the following *types* of resources you'll need to complete each work package—human, facilities, equipment, materials and supplies, and "special" resources:

TIP

Use project team members and contributors to brainstorm a list of all the resources you'll need to complete this project. Then identify which resources will be required for each work package.

- Human resources identifies specific professional and technical skills and the knowledge and experience the work package will require.

- Facilities refers to the specific type of location, space, or work area required (physical plant).

- Equipment represents the tools, machines, or systems needed (electrical or mechanical and reusable).

- Materials and supplies are the raw materials, purchased goods, parts, sub-assemblies, supplies, books, or documents required (consumables).

- Special resources refer to anything that might not be commonly available in your organization and that could require special effort to obtain. For example, if a compact disc manufacturer needed gold to complete a project, it might be considered a special resource since it's not something the organization uses regularly.

Not all of these resources will come from within your organization. If you need to explore outside vendors, it's important to know more about contracts. (See Contracts for Survival on page 51.)

Once you've identified the type of resources you'll need to complete each work package, you can determine the *amount* of each resource the work package will require. For example, look at work package 3.1 in Example 2.4 on pages 43–44. For knowledge and skills, the project team determined it would require two people with electrical skills working for three days for a total of 48 hours (based on the assumption that it would take one hour to hook up each workstation); and someone from facilities to oversee the work. For materials, it was determined that electrical wiring (cable and connectors) would be needed for 48 workstations.

Frequently Forgotten Resource Requirements

Have you ever left for a long business trip or vacation, only to be plagued by the feeling that you've forgotten something? Well, before embarking on your project management journey, make sure you include all resource requirements—even ones that project managers most often forget. Here are a few to consider:

- Cost-of-living adjustments, especially if the project has a lengthy time line

- Off-site differentials (labor and material costs may differ significantly in other locations)

- Equipment costs to perform or measure special operations

- License, permit, or certification costs

- Tariffs and duties

- Currency exchange

- Rush charges

- Overtime

- Documentation and reporting

- Planned prework

Now that you've determined the type and amount of each resource needed for each work package, you'll need to estimate the total *cost*. Do this by multiplying the cost per unit of a specific type of resource by the amount of units needed. For example, if a work package calls for someone with "database administration skills" to spend 18 person-days, and the cost is $400 per day, then the total cost for this resource would be $7,200 (18 × $400 = $7,200). Example 2.4 (pp. 43–44) displays the resource or skill needed, percentage of time allocated to each work package, and a cost estimate.

TIP

If you make assumptions when estimating the type, amount, or cost of resources, document them in the WBS dictionary and attempt to confirm them with experts or stakeholders.

When you estimate the time you'll need for human resources, use units that represent actual *time-on-task* rather than the overall duration of the task. For example, if you'll need a

Example 2.4 Resource Requirements

Work Packages	Knowledge/Skills				Facilities				Equipment				Notes
	Type	Amount	Unit Cost	Total Cost	Type	Amount	Unit Cost	Total Cost	Type	Amount	Unit Cost	Total Cost	
2.3 Office interior designed	Interior design skills	1 × 4 days = 32 hrs	$150 per hr	$4,800									Assumes designers will want to tour site
	Facilities management skills	1 × 2 days = 16 hrs	$0	$0									Assumes 3 department mgrs.
	Department knowledge	3 × ¾ day = 6 hrs	$0	$0									
	Project management skills	1 × ¼ day = 2 hrs	$0	$0									
	Engineering skills	1 × ¼ day = 2 hrs	$0	$0									
2.4 Equipment and office furnishings ordered	Purchasing skills	1 × ½ day = 4 hrs	$0	$0					Workstations	12	N/A	$70,000	Assumes 12 new workstations.
	Facilities management skills	1 × ¼ day = 2 hrs	$0	$0									
2.5 Equipment and office furnishings received	Receiving/storing skills	1 × 1 day = 8 hrs	$0	$0									
	Facilities management skills	1 × ¼ day = 2 hrs	$0	$0									
3.1 Electrical services installed	Electrical skills	2 × 3 days = 48 hrs	$65 per hr	$3,120									
	Facilities management skills	1 × ½ day = 4 hrs	$0	$0									
Totals				$7,920				$0				$70,000	

(continued)

Example 2.4 Continued

Work Packages	Materials				Special Resources					Notes
	Type	Amount	Unit Cost	Total Cost	Type	Amount	Unit Cost	Total Cost	$	
2.3 Office interior designed					Travel/ Entertainment			$250	$ 5,050	Assumes designers will want to tour site. Assumes 3 department managers.
2.4 Equipment and office furnishings ordered	Purchase orders	N/A	N/A	$0					$70,000	Assumes 12 new work-stations. $70,000 is a discounted price.
2.5 Equipment and office furnishings received										
3.1 Electrical services installed	Electrical wiring	N/A	N/A	$6,000					$ 9,120	Assumes electrical wiring service for 48 work stations and 1 work station per hour to wire. Assumes 2 electricians. Assumes cabling runs and connections for 48 workstations.
Totals				$6,000				$250	$84,170	

The Guess Work in Estimating

Identifying resource requirements requires you to estimate how much of those resources you will need. The three generally accepted estimating methods for project management are:

1. *Analogous*—You establish a total cost based on the typical cost of similar projects and then assign a percentage of the costs across the major deliverables. This estimate is developed to test the available budget.

2. *Detailed*—You establish the total cost by adding the cost of all the work packages.

3. *Parametric*—You use accepted norms for incremental pricing to obtain the estimate. For example, it will cost 20¢ per square foot to carpet your office.

There are also three different types of estimates you can produce. The type you choose should depend first on how rigorous you need to be to satisfy project stakeholders and then on how rigorous you need to be for planning purposes.

1. *Order of Magnitude*—Primarily used for determining project feasibility (accurate from −25% to +75%). This is calculated at the major deliverable level.

2. *Budget*—Relies on previous project data and benchmarking, and is used for general planning and budgeting (accurate from −10% to +25%). Budgets are calculated at the sub-deliverable level.

3. *Definitive*—Based on the detailed work plans and resource charts, and used to manage project performance (accurate from −5% to +10%). A definitive estimate is calculated at the work package level.

---

technical writer for four hours a day, two days a week over the course of three weeks, the total time will be 24 hours ($4 \times 2 \times 3 = 24$), not three weeks.

To complete your cost estimate, total the resource costs for each work package, then total the resource costs for each major deliverable. Finally, total all of the major deliverables to determine overall project cost.

TIP

You need to account for a resource's time on your project even if your organization does not account for their internal billing rate. This will help with scheduling from a limited pool of resources that is required to support several projects.

Alternatively, it may be important to total resource costs by type. For example, you may want to separate total equipment costs if they represent a cash outlay as compared to human resources that will be accounted for only as an internal billing charge to the project.

Identifying resource requirements will help you assess the total effort required to complete the project—giving you, as well as management and other project stakeholders, an understanding of the true cost of the project. In addition, outlining resource requirements at the beginning of a project will provide you with a basis for controlling project costs and monitoring resource use during implementation. It is the starting point for establishing the *code of accounts* or *chart of accounts*. These terms refer to the numbering system that will identify and track cost for each work package by type of expense, such as labor, materials, equipment, and so on. Your organization's finance or accounting department may have a chart of accounts in place that apply here.

Join Together

Once again, you should rely on your project team and experienced project managers for input. However, also include the human resources themselves as well as their managers, since they usually have the best estimates as to how much time and effort it will take to complete their piece of the project. Including your resources will help you gain their commitment to the project. Involving the managers will enhance their willingness to release the resources to your project.

In addition, include experts who can provide initial estimates and validate estimates based on experience. Historical documents and commercial cost-estimating databases can also be helpful, if you have access to them.

It may also be useful to divide identifying resource requirements into two rounds. In the first round, you'll calculate an initial estimate with the help of others. In the second round, you'll review the initial estimate with the same resources, as well as with others who can spot inaccuracies, oversights, or shortcuts.

The More You Know . . .

You may want to do a cost/benefit analysis before implementing your project. Once you've established the overall cost of the project, you'll be able to compare it with the value described in the project statement and objectives. This will confirm whether you should continue defining and planning the project, whether adjustments need to be made, or whether the project should be completely rethought, delayed, or abandoned.

If adjustments need to be made at the work package level, examine the work packages and ask:

- How does this work package help us reach our objectives?
- Can we eliminate this work package and still meet the objectives?
- Is the cost for this work package greater than the value it delivers?
- Does this work package create more value, functionality, or reliability than is needed?
- Is there an alternative way to accomplish or complete this work package so that it has a better benefit-for-cost ratio?

TIP

You also need to understand the burden rates for work groups and departments. Many salaried organizations can only come to terms with human resource capacity constraints when they see the financial implications of adding more projects to their portfolio.

There's also the possibility that you'll choose between several alternatives when selecting a resource. If this is the case, there are a number of variables to consider, including things like:

- Geographic locations
- Transportation options
- Local/federal laws and regulations
- Organizational policies and procedures
- Industry best practices

- Political dynamics
- Availability of resources
- Time needed to acquire new capabilities

For more information on making a decision, see page 181 for a description of Decision Analysis.

Dealing with uncertainty is almost unavoidable when it comes to estimating the amount and cost of resources. Therefore, many project managers tend to *overestimate* to ensure that they don't "blow the budget." After all, it's much easier to explain why you performed under the budget than why you overshot your mark.

Common methods for preparing for the unexpected include contingency planning, backup resources, and reserve funds. All three (and there are others) basically refer to built-in space to accommodate the unexpected. Some project managers increase the amount of particular resources needed; others increase the duration of specific tasks; and still others use multipliers to pad their estimates. In some organizations, a contingency fund is established in case resource estimates prove inaccurate, significant changes in scope occur, or unanticipated threats alter the project plan. However, a project manager must present clear, documented reasons for tapping reserve funds, and, often, approval must come from management.

The best way to handle uncertainty isn't to randomly pad your resource requirements. Rather, it's to examine the likelihood that an estimate will be inaccurate, the potential magnitude of the difference, and what the impact will be on the overall project (and organization) if it's incorrect. For example, estimating resources and costs associated with work packages that have not been done before will probably have a high likelihood of being inaccurate. In this case, you may want to overestimate. For more information on planning for what could go wrong, see Protect and Enhance the Plan on page 82.

PITFALL

Don't overestimate just to avoid rigorous estimating. Overestimating work package requirements without precise calculation can result in an inaccurate overall estimate. This could threaten the approval of the project, or occupy resources that could be better spent elsewhere.

ADDITIONAL DEFINITION TOPICS

Choose to Win: Selecting a Project Manager

Organizations around the world embrace project management as the way they accomplish work. Not surprisingly, the role of the project manager has become increasingly critical, and the demands and responsibilities of the job have grown.

As a project manager, you're sensitive to the needs of the project, and smart enough to sell it to senior management and other stakeholders. You work effectively with theoretical-minded scientists and researchers while still staying within the budget. And you balance the differing schedules and workstyles of creative individuals like graphic designers and software programmers with the need to meet deadlines. Sound a bit like a superhero?

Selecting a project manager demands a careful, rational process. Choosing the right project manager might mean the difference between a successful project and a failure.

Each project is unique and will require specific selection criteria. However, there are several generic criteria that will get you started. In general, a project manager should have:

- Management skills for team building, negotiating, delegating responsibility, managing performance, managing the involvement of others, and conducting project communication
- Technical knowledge and skills relevant to the project
- Project management skills
- Problem-solving and decision-making skills
- Commitment to the project's success
- Support from their manager
- Time to devote to the project
- Ability to develop a working relationship with team members and other stakeholders

For more information on establishing objectives to help you decide on which project manager to pick, see Decision Analysis on page 181.

Splitting Projects into Subprojects

Most project managers prefer to maintain control over all aspects of their projects; relinquishing a major deliverable or two can carry a negative connotation because it implies that they can't handle the work. Not true. In fact, determining whether part of your project should be managed separately is often necessary if you want to complete the overall project on time and within budget. Subprojects can be done within an organization, or completely delegated to an outside vendor or contractor.

Complex or lengthy projects often require subprojects to group or manage activities that are similar in nature, share resources, share funding, or have constraints that require they be done together.

Here's a list of questions to help you decide whether to split your project into two or more subprojects:

- Is the overall project too large or complex for a single person to manage effectively? If so, consider separating it.
- Does work for one part of the project require specialized knowledge? Specialized or technical work may require a sub-project manager with skills or knowledge in that area.
- Should resources be managed differently for parts of the project? It's often best to manage work together if it requires the same type of resources or special cost accounting.
- Is someone needed to sponsor a part of the project? Grouping work together that shares a need for the same special influence can help expedite the process.

Once you've sliced off a subproject, treat it like a mini-project. Assign a separate subproject manager; develop a statement, objectives, and WBS; review the resource requirements; then, follow the remaining steps and activities in this book. Remember to keep the project objectives for the subproject consistent with the overall project objectives. It may require additional or different monitoring, and the subproject manager may choose to add more detail to the WBS, responsibility assignments, and schedule.

Contracts for Survival

If you decide to use an outside vendor to provide a resource or handle a work package or subproject, first study the types of contracts available:

- *Firm fixed price* (FFP): The vendor will only receive the agreed price, regardless of any unanticipated cost or schedule overruns.

- *Firm price incentive fee* (FPIF): The vendor receives the agreed price plus a bonus for on-time or early completion.

- *Cost plus incentive fee* (CPIF): The vendor receives actual costs to provide the goods or services plus a bonus for on-time or early completion.

- *Cost plus fixed fee* (CPFF): The vendor receives actual costs plus a guaranteed fee, even if the project is not completed.

- *Cost plus award fee* (CPAF): The vendor receives actual costs plus an award based on performance against some quality indicator(s).

Your choice will depend on the goods or services being provided, as well as the financial risk involved (for the vendor as well as your organization). Obviously, firm fixed price (FFP) contracts are high-risk for the vendor and low-risk for the customer. Conversely, cost plus award fee (CPAF) contracts place most of the potential risk with the customer and very little with the vendor. The others represent risk ratios somewhere between those extremes. The type of contract chosen should reflect several things, including:

- The degree of difficulty in providing the goods or services.
- Whether it involves hazardous materials or methods.
- Whether there will be future use for the goods or services.
- Whether the deliverable is well defined and unlikely to change.

Contractor-Customer Risk

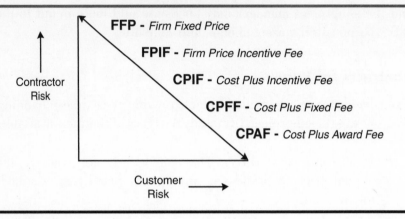

Contractor Risk

FFP - *Firm Fixed Price*

FPIF - *Firm Price Incentive Fee*

CPIF - *Cost Plus Incentive Fee*

CPFF - *Cost Plus Fixed Fee*

CPAF - *Cost Plus Award Fee*

Customer Risk →

Select the contract that represents risk that is acceptable to both the vendor and your organization. Your organization's legal, contracting, and purchasing departments may have policies and procedures in place that apply here.

TIP

In some countries, the government or other agencies provide incentives for hiring nontraditional subcontractors. Project managers should examine their project plans for opportunities where such subcontractors could be best utilized.

Assessing the Financials

Cost is often a critical factor in projects. The money spent should be considered as an investment, and a reasonable return should be expected. The worth of the investment is often the deciding factor for whether a project gets done or which among several possible projects deserves allocation of limited resources. Organizations typically use several methods to assess a project's financial soundness.

Payout time is one method of evaluating the investment. This method compares all the project expenses to the expected net income by time period (e.g., by month or year), and finds the point when the investment will be repaid. Capital is not included in the expenses because it does not represent worth that leaves the organization. Cash spent on capital is simply converted to physical and durable goods retained within the organization. Project income is in the form of revenue or savings produced from the project. Organizations often have set standards for payout time. For example, a policy may state that no project will be approved with a projected payout time of more than one year.

Return on investment (ROI) is the ratio of annual profit to the investment in the project. The average annual profit produced by the income is divided by the total project investment. Multiplying this number by 100 represents the ratio as a percentage. To calculate ROI, capital is included in the project expenses, since it represents money that could be invested elsewhere. Any depreciation expected on that capital must also be subtracted from the annual profit. Many organizations use ROI to compare projects competing for the same investment or to test against a set minimum return that any project must outperform.

Net present value (NPV) calculates how much value a project will produce beyond an expected return, should the investment be retained in another minimally acceptable form. For example, an organization may have a choice between keeping cash invested in a certificate of deposit returning 10 percent, or putting it into a project. NPV calculates how much more cash the project will return than if the cash were kept in the certificate of deposit. This is calculated using the following formula:

$$NPV = \frac{\text{Year 1 income}}{(1 + \text{Accepted return})^1} + \frac{\text{Year } n \text{ income}}{(1 + \text{Accepted return})^n} - \text{Investment}$$

Internal rate of return (IRR) considers the time value of money. In other words, it factors in not only the return but also how quickly it will be realized. It shows this as a discount rate that makes the expected returns equal to the current investment. This rate can be compared to the rates earned by investing the money in other projects or investments. If the project requires borrowing, an organization will usually insist that it must earn an IRR that is at least several percentage points higher than the cost of borrowing to compensate for the risk, time, and trouble associated with the project. For example, consider a project costing $7,500 and expected to return $2,000 per year for five years, or $10,000 total. The IRR calculated for the project would be 10 percent. If the cost of borrowing is less than 10 percent, the project may be justified. If the cost of borrowing is 10 percent or greater, the project will break even at best. The easiest way to calculate IRR is to use a financial calculator or present value tables. If the income is uneven each year, IRR can be calculated by trial and error, using different rates in the following formula, until the rate equals the expected return.

$$\text{Investment} = \frac{\text{Year 1 income}}{(1 + RR)^1} + \frac{\text{Year } n \text{ income}}{(1 + RR)^n}$$

Definition Summary

Definition serves as the precursor to Planning and Implementation. It's here that the scope and reasons for completing the project become clear to the project team, project stakeholders, and contributors. It's the time when you begin to gain commitment from these groups. It's also the time when the organization decides to link its resources to the objectives it's trying to achieve.

In *The Modern Theme*, José Ortega y Gasset wrote "To define is to exclude and negate" (translated from Spanish by James Cleugh, W. W. Norton, New York, 1933, p. 99). Although he intended a negative connotation, you might agree that his words apply to the work done during project definition. To define your project is to specify its purpose and scope, excluding everything else. Or, as the anonymous sculptor said, "When I sculpt a statue of an elephant, I take a block of stone and chip away everything that doesn't look like an elephant."

chapter
3

project planning

*I*T WAS A STRUGGLE, *but they did it. Under Tim's (the project manager's) direction, the project team outlined the project statement and objectives, and assembled a work breakdown structure (WBS) with resource require- ments. The group feels satisfied with their accomplishments to date, but their excitement is dulled by the Planning activities lurking before them. Their challenge is to create a project plan that balances resource avail- ability with resource needs, minimizes scheduling conflicts, arranges the work in the appropriate sequence, and accomplishes all of this without major schedule or cost problems.*

In this latest meeting, Tim starts posing questions to the group: Who is actually going to do the office layouts? Whose approval is needed for them? Who has primary responsibility for working with the movers? Which moving company will they hire? How much time will the movers need? Who needs to supervise the installation of the new furniture? Should the furniture be in hand before the office area is prepared? What could go wrong in any of these steps?

The team feels buried, but Tim guides them through the planning process using questions in a step-by-step format.

How will you do the work?

In Definition, you established why you were doing this project, and you wrote a project statement and objectives to capture and formalize your reasoning. You also recorded how the work needed to be accomplished to achieve these goals by developing a WBS. Now, you'll create a plan to actually complete the work you've identified.

During Planning, you'll ask five questions:

1. Who will be responsible for each work package in the WBS?
2. In what order should (or must) the work packages be accomplished, and how much time will it take to complete each work package?
3. How should the project be scheduled against a calendar?
4. Are enough resources available when needed?
5. What problems or opportunities may occur during the project, and what can be done now to plan for them?

During Planning, you'll gain an understanding of who will do what and when.

Five project management Planning activities will structure your answers:

1. Assign Responsibility
2. Sequence Deliverables
3. Schedule Deliverables
4. Schedule Resources
5. Protect and Enhance the Plan

ASSIGN RESPONSIBILITY

TIP
What if you assign responsibility to individuals who have more capability than you need? Or, alternatively, what will you do if you assign responsibility to people with less-than-ideal experience, skills, or ability? In either case, you'll need to re-estimate cost and time-on-task.

A work package, like any form of work, will have a higher likelihood of being completed if you formally assign it to a specific individual or group. Work left unassigned is often overlooked, forgotten, or dropped because of the "I-thought-you-were-going-to-do-it" syndrome.

Therefore, assigning responsibility for each work package is the first activity in Planning.

To assign responsibility, examine each work package in your WBS, as well as the knowledge and skills necessary to complete it (you documented these resources when you identified resource requirements). Then, ask the following questions:

- Who has the knowledge, skills, expertise, information, or experience to complete this work package?
- Who will provide the resources (facilities, equipment, materials and supplies, special requirements) you need to complete this work package?
- Who needs to approve, commit to, or review this work package?

The answers will identify specific names and responsibilities associated with each work package. One of the most effective tools for charting this information is the *Responsibility Assignment Matrix* (RAM).

Tool: Responsibility Assignment Matrix

Construct a RAM to match people with work packages. A RAM is a chart that lists work packages along its vertical axis and individuals or groups along its horizontal axis. Within each cell are listed the activities that the individual or group is responsible for. In Example 3.1, the first column lists deliverable 2. (Office equipment) from the WBS, as well as its related work packages. The remaining columns list the departments, teams, or individuals who will contribute to this project.

PITFALL

Don't forget government regulations (local, state, and federal laws) and labor agreements. These factors can influence how you staff your project, the number of hours you assign to individuals, and how much their time will cost. Considering them during Planning will save rework and potential legal ramifications later in the project.

Decide each person's or group's responsibilities: Will they be reviewing work, making sure resources are in place, preparing a facility, creating a product, facilitating a meeting, writing a press release, conducting interviews, producing a report, designing a part, and so on? Record this information in the corresponding RAM cell. Your RAM should also identify the person who has *primary responsibility* for completing the work package. In Example 3.1, that person is identified with a (P). Identifying someone with

Example 3.1 Responsibility Assignment Matrix

Project Statement

Move the Corporate Customer Services Department within three months at a cost not to exceed $170,000.

Work Breakdown Structure	Project Manager	Facilities Manager	Purchasing Coordinator	Department Managers	Receiving Clerk	Engineer	Interior Decorator	Senior Vice President
2. Office Equipment								
2.1 Equipment to keep identified	Provide input, as needed	Recommend a list of equipment to keep (P)		Approve equipment to keep for own department	Check transportation cost	Check compatibility, usability, safety issues		
2.2 Equipment to order identified	Monitor cost and availability of equipment	Recommend a list of equipment to order (P)	Check availability of equipment with potential vendors	Approve the equipment list		Provide input, as needed		
2.3 Office interior designed	Review recommendation and design	Recommend an interior decorator; Get design approved (P)		Approve recommendation and design		Review recommendation and design	Submit detailed design plans	
2.4 Equipment and office furnishings ordered			Submit purchase orders for equipment and furnishings (P)					Approve purchase orders
2.5 Equipment and office furnishings received	Monitor arrival date				Receive and store equipment and furnishings (P)			

(P) Designates primary responsibility; others have secondary responsibilities.

primary responsibility will reduce misunderstandings among the team and other contributors and will help you monitor progress more effectively. Only one person should have primary responsibility for a work package. All others have secondary responsibility.

Take time to assign responsibility for your work packages using a RAM or an equivalent tool. This will establish clear ownership of all tasks required to successfully complete the project. It will also involve project communication to secure commitment of project contributors and the approval of their managers.

Join Together

Assigning responsibility often occurs over the course of several rounds of negotiation. These rounds can take place during one meeting or occur over several conversations. The first round, called the *initial work negotiation*, involves you (the project manager) and the provider(s) of primary resources (*resource or functional managers*).

TIP

Remember the additional, secondary resources you identified? Obtaining their time may not require a formal work negotiation, but you should still approach them (and their managers) to negotiate their time and secure their commitment.

Sometimes, the resource manager is the individual who will be assigned the work package; in other cases, the resource manager is the manager of the individual(s) you need. Regardless, there are generally four topics that should be addressed during the initial work negotiation:

1. How appropriate are task and performance expectations for the designated individual?

2. How available are that individual to work on the project?

3. How realistic are the budget and timing?

4. How committed is the resource provider?

TIP

When negotiating for resources, remember to separate the people from the issue; focus on the issue and not the individual positions; examine various alternatives to resolve the issue; and insist on using a set of objectives to help guide the discussion.

After you gain their commitment, the resources become project contributors. Even so, you'll continue negotiations throughout Planning and Implementation regarding their time and availability.

You'll also need to agree on what's expected of project contributors. This round of project communication will involve you, the contributors, and their managers. In this round, you and the individual agree (with the manager's input) to *performance expectations.* (See Influencing People on page 133 for information on the Performance System and setting performance expectations.) Use the following questions as a checklist to ensure you prepare the resource properly for the task at hand. Discuss your answers in the meeting:

(See Influencing People on page 133 for information on the Performance System and setting performance expectations.)

- What exactly is expected as an outcome of the work packages assigned to the contributor?
- Does the contributor understand what is expected and agree to it?
- Is the contributor capable of meeting the expectations?
- Will the contributor's work environment support performance on this project?
- How will the performance of the contributor be measured?
- What is the relative priority of this work compared to other projects and work the contributor is assigned to?

TIP

You will receive the best performance from those contributors who not only understand and agree to your expectations but who also have a genuine interest in the project and stand to receive positive consequences from their involvement. Clarify the benefits of working on your project, and try to align contributors with tasks they actually *want* to perform.

PITFALL

Do not try to set measures or standards for every activity of each work package. It will bog you down. Select the most important activities, especially those that may still be unclear to the resource provider, and flesh out expectations for them. As for the rest, verbal agreements, ground rules, or rules of thumb should suffice.

In Example 3.2, performance expectations have been set for one activity that the facilities manager will undertake in order to complete work package 2.3 (Office interior designed). Before the office interior can be designed, an interior decorator has to be hired. The decision has to be approved by the department managers. There are certain requirements or aspects of performance of the activity that will be measured. These are

Example 3.2 Performance Expectations for the Facilities Manager

Work Breakdown Structure	Activity	Requirements	Measures	Standards
2. Office Equipment				
2.3 Office interior designed	Recommend an interior decorator.	Quantity	Number of interior decorators evaluated.	Evaluate at least 4.
		Quality	Degree to which interior decorators evaluated meet decision criteria.	Two best choices must meet at least 80% of all Want objectives.
		Timeliness	Time to complete the Decision Analysis.	No more than 3 days.
		Cost	Cost involved in making the decision (gathering data, setting objectives, touring the facilities).	No more than $250.

typically in the area of quality, quantity, timeliness, and cost. A measure indicates how you will assess performance against the requirements; standards set the specific level of performance that is expected.

The More You Know . . .

You may require a specific individual who is not readily available to contribute to your project. Ask yourself how critical it is for this particular individual to complete this particular work package. If you decide the resource is irreplaceable, it could mean you have to shift your project schedule to accommodate the resource or resume negotiations to release some

PITFALL

When you negotiate, consider the viewpoint of the resource provider. He or she may be short-staffed, overworked, or face negative consequences for releasing a resource to you. Negotiating with this in mind will increase your chances of securing the resource you want or at least gaining the next best alternative.

of his or her time (you'll make this type of decision during the Schedule Resources activity).

If you decide someone else will suffice, you'll need to select a new person and conduct another Initial Work Negotiation. Consider the answers to these questions as you choose the best replacement:

- What objectives will the alternate resource need to satisfy to be acceptable?

- What restrictions, policies, procedures, or standards must be considered?

- Can this individual be developed to better meet project requirements?

SEQUENCE DELIVERABLES

You've identified *who* will be responsible for the project work. Now you need to determine the order in which the work packages should be completed, how long each will take to finish, and the total duration of the project.

Arrange the work packages in the order you will accomplish them. Some work packages must be completed before others can be started, while others can be done at the same time. Review the relationships in Example 3.3; they're identified in the column labeled "Precedence Relationships." Work package 1.1.2 (Relationship charts drawn) shouldn't start until 1.1.1 (Interviews conducted) is completed. Likewise, work packages 2.1, 2.2, and 2.3 must precede work package 2.4 (Equipment and office furnishings ordered). Identify relationships between all work packages, then arrange them in a table as shown in Example 3.3. This is called a *precedence table*.

TIP

It's tempting to position work packages in linear order. ("First, we will do this; then, we will do that; next, we will accomplish this.") However, finding ways to complete work packages simultaneously will reduce overall project duration as long as they don't compete for resources.

As you organize your work packages, you'll discover several different kinds of precedence relationships. Some work packages have a

Example 3.3   Precedence Table

Project Statement

Move the Corporate Customer Services Department within three months at a cost not to exceed $170,000.

Work Packages	Precedence Relationships	Duration
1.1.1 Interviews conducted	None	3 days
1.1.2 Relationship charts drawn	After 1.1.1	2 days
1.2 Department block layouts drawn	After 1.1.2	2 days
1.3 Department detailed layouts drawn	After 1.2	4 days
2.1 Equipment to keep identified	After 1.3	1 day
2.2 Equipment to order identified	After 1.3	1 day
2.3 Office interior designed	After 1.3	8 days
2.4 Equipment and office furnishings ordered	After 2.1, 2.2, 2.3	1 day
2.5. Equipment and office furnishings received	After 2.4	11 days*
3.1 Electrical services installed	After 1.3	3 days

*Ten days to fill order, 1 day to receive and store.

mandatory (hard logic) dependency on one another; for example, a house cannot be framed unless the foundation is finished. Other work packages have a *best-practice (preferential) relationship.* For example, it's more efficient to run electrical wires *after* plumbing has been installed. It's also possible that some work packages have *discretionary dependency,* that is, they're arranged in a certain order because the customer or project manager wants it that way. For example, the owner of the house wants the driveway completed before the deck is built. And, finally, some work packages have an *external relationship,* meaning that they have a relationship with activities outside the project that dictate the order of their completion. For example, if major road construction (not related to your project) will cut off access to your building site, you may want to complete certain work packages earlier to avoid this threat.

The Order of the Day

You can use four types of precedence relationships to determine how work packages should be ordered:

1. *Finish-to-Start*—Simplest, most commonly used technique; refers to finishing work package A before starting work package B. (e.g., Finish hiring the operator before starting to train the operator.)

2. *Finish-to-Finish*—Finish A in order to finish B. (e.g., Finish final customer-requirements meeting to finish documenting the requirements.)

3. *Start-to-Start*—Start A in order to start B. (e.g., Start writing the book before starting to edit the book.)

4. *Start-to-Finish*—Start A in order to finish B. (e.g., Start project manager selection process to finish the proposal development process.)

Determine the duration of each work package from start to finish, given the caliber and availability of resources. Your estimate should represent *elapsed time* of each work package, not actual time-on-task. (You calculated time-on-task in Identify Resource Requirements.)

TIP

Did you make any assumptions when estimating elapsed time? If so, remember to record them in your WBS dictionary, along with plans to check or confirm your assumptions later.

For example, review work package 2.5 (Equipment and office furnishings received) in Example 3.3. The time-on-task to receive the office equipment is one day. However, the duration, or elapsed time, for the supplier to fill the order is 10 days, making the total duration for that work package 11 days. Record the duration for each work package in a table (see Example 3.3) or enter it directly into your project management software. Another way to estimate duration is to examine the availability of a specific resource. If time-on-task of a work package is 10 days, and you have two resources who can work on this but only at the rate of one day a week, your total duration will be five weeks.

As you finalize the elapsed time of a task, keep in mind there is often a need to add *lag time*. Lag time refers to the necessary, built-in gap between the timing of two work packages. For example, if you paint a room as one work package and hang framed pictures as the next work package, you'll need to add lag time for the paint to dry. You could include this lag time as part of the work package's duration, or you could build a gap between work packages. Either way, you need to have sufficient time between when the actual paint work finishes and the work of hanging the pictures starts to allow for drying time.

Using this information, you'll be able to estimate the total duration of the project. There are several tools that will help improve your accuracy in this calculation.

Tools: Network Diagrams

For small projects, relying on your precedence table and a simple network diagram will be sufficient for demonstrating project flow and calculating project duration.

Construct a *network diagram* based on your precedence table. A network diagram is a common method of demonstrating the sequence of work packages in a project plan. Using a combination of arrows (→) and nodes (○), you can graphically depict the flow of the project from start to finish.

On the left side of the page, draw a start node, and, on the right, a finish node. Software frequently uses rectangles to represent nodes. Represent each work package with a node, and use arrows to show the relationship from one work package to another. In Example 3.4, work package 4. (System installed) cannot be started until work package 2. (System purchased) has been completed, and work package 2. cannot begin until both work packages 6. (Region offices contacted) and 1. (System designed) are completed. Review your network to ensure that every node, with the exception of the start and finish nodes, has at

TIP

Don't add extra time to the critical path to ensure an on-time finish. For example, on a 20-work-package project, if everyone has an extra day added as a precaution, you may increase your project's duration significantly. It's better to evaluate individual work packages to uncover specific potential problems that might cause delays. (See "Protect and Enhance the Plan" on page 82 for more information on identifying and preparing for potential problems.)

Example 3.4   Activity-on-Node or Precedence Diagramming Method

Work Packages	Precedents
1. System designed	None
2. System purchased	1, 6
3. Personnel trained (at vendor site)	1
4. System installed	2
5. System pilot tested	3, 4
6. Region offices contacted	None

least one entering and one exiting arrow. This representation of the precedence table is called *activity-on-node* diagram. You may also be asked to use an *activity-on-arrow* diagram. See Example 3.5, in which the arrows represent work packages and the nodes represent starts and finishes. This type of diagram sometimes contains dummy activities. Such an activity indicates a precedence relationship but does not consume resources. It is shown by a broken arrow. Example 3.6 illustrates a detailed network diagram for the Corporate Customer Services office move.

To reveal the minimum amount of time it will take to complete the entire project, find the path that represents the *most* elapsed time

Example 3.5   Activity-on-Arrow or Arrow Diagramming Method

Work Packages	Precedents
1. System designed	None
2. System purchased	1, 6
3. Personnel trained (at vendor site)	1
4. System installed	2
5. System pilot tested	3, 4
6. Region offices contacted	None
Dummy task	1

through the network diagram and has no slack. This is the *critical path* because it represents the minimum elapsed time required to complete your project. If something impacts the duration of work packages on this path, it will directly impact the finish date of the entire project. (See More about Critical Path on page 90.)

Look at Example 3.6. The critical path is highlighted. Add up the duration of the work packages on the critical path, and you'll see that

Example 3.6   Activity-on-Node Network Diagram

Project Statement

Move the Corporate Customer Services Department within three months at a cost not to exceed $170,000.

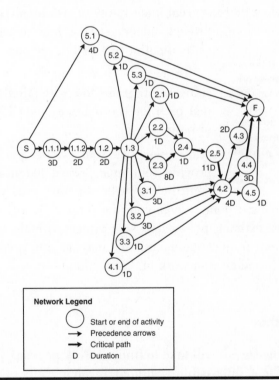

Project Statement

Move the Corporate Customer Services department within three months at a cost not to exceed $170,000

it's 38 days—the longest path. If your estimates are accurate, it's also the least amount of time it will take to complete the entire project.

One network technique is called the *Critical Path Method* (CPM). In this method, you assign each work package a *single* duration estimate that you and your team believe is the most probable duration. Then add up the duration of all work packages on the critical path to calculate the time it should take to finish your project. (For how to calculate the critical path using CPM, see page 91.)

The *Program Evaluation and Review Technique* (PERT) is another network technique. It uses a statistical approach to calculating the probability of work packages being completed on time. With PERT, you and your project team assign three duration estimates to each work package: optimistic, most likely, and pessimistic. Then, using a weighted average of the three estimates, you calculate the shortest time to complete the project. PERT calculations are useful when there are significant variations in optimistic and pessimistic estimates and when there is great uncertainty or risk involved regarding project outcomes. (For how to calculate the critical path using PERT, see page 95.)

PITFALL

Look at the length of the other paths in your network. If they are nearly as long as the critical path, they will need to be monitored carefully. Slippages on these paths could change your critical path.

There are many project management software programs that will calculate the critical path for you using either CPM or PERT or both.

Sequencing your work packages will provide you, your project team, and project contributors with the order in which work packages must get done to complete the project. It will also offer a more accurate estimate of how long your project will take to complete. Remember your project statement? You may need to revise the completion date based on your work in this section.

Join Together

Estimating the time it will take to finish a work package will be very difficult—if not impossible—without involving others, especially those individuals whom you've assigned to handle them. Make sure you involve contributors, project team members, and others who have managed or contributed to similar projects in the past.

They can also advise you and your team on whether work packages must be done sequentially or can be done concurrently, and on the validity and accuracy of your network diagram assumptions.

The More You Know . . .

You may be involved in managing a project that requires a change in direction or a repetition of steps. If this is the case, consider using the *Graphical Evaluation and Review Technique* (GERT). This is a network technique that is similar to PERT but has the advantage of allowing you to omit certain portions of the network, complete certain work packages partially, or repeat certain work packages several times. This technique allows for looping, in which the network path passes through the same node more than once (e.g., clinical trials that must be repeated several times). It also allows for branching, in which the network path can split in one of two or more directions depending on the results of an event or work package (e.g., design changes if a product fails testing). (See Example 3.7.)

Example 3.7   Network with Probabilistic Branching and Looping

Work Packages	Precedents
1. Position advertised	None
2. Résumés screened	1
3. Interviews conducted	2
4. Offer accepted	3

SCHEDULE DELIVERABLES

You've estimated the duration and set the sequence of each work package, and determined the approximate length of the entire project. Now it's time to link work packages with actual start and finish calendar dates.

Using the precedence and duration work you did in Sequence Deliverables, follow these steps:

TIP

Don't assign aggressive start and finish dates without sound reasoning. Although it's usually better to pursue a schedule that completes the project quickly, compare the benefits of speed with its risks and potential adverse consequences.

- Select the project start date.

- Identify all nonworking days (i.e., company holidays, weekends, vacation days) on the calendar.

- Identify any date constraints that were surfaced during objectives setting or initial work negotiations.

- Schedule a start and end date for each work package and record them on a time line or calendar.

- Identify the overall completion date.

Keep the following in mind when scheduling your project:

- Schedule all work packages to begin as soon as possible. If you schedule them to begin as late as possible, all work packages will become critical, even those that have *slack time.* Slack time (also called *float* or *total float*) is the amount of time that a work package can be delayed from its early start without delaying the project's finish date. *Free float* is the amount of time that a work package can be delayed without affecting the early start of work packages immediately succeeding it. Critical path work packages do not have slack time.

- You and your project team may be forced to deal with a predetermined completion date (e.g., the date the lease expires on your organization's rented office space). In such cases, find out the absolute latest date your project must start by "moving" backward from the completion date until you arrive at the start date. This will help you determine whether you can complete the project on time and whether you need to start immediately or add additional resources.

- As you schedule your project, you could uncover slack time. For example, one of your work packages that must be finished by January 14 cannot start until January 6 because the work it depends on will not be completed until close of business on January 5. Since this work package will require three days to finish, the latest you can start is January 11. You have five days of slack time for this work package. (To uncover the slack time for a specific work package, calculate the difference between the earliest start and finish time and the latest start and finish time. To learn how to do this, see More about Critical Path on page 90.) Use slack time to help match resources with work packages.

TIP

Take into account nonworking days (like holidays and weekends) when you schedule deliverables.

Tool: Gantt Chart

As you learned in Sequence Deliverables, a table is often the most effective tool for communicating work package duration and precedence when it comes to small projects. A table can also display work package start and end dates for a small project.

However, as the size and complexity of your project increases, consider plotting your start and finish dates on a *Gantt chart*. A Gantt chart is a graph that uses horizontal bars to represent the project time line. To construct a Gantt chart, record work packages on the vertical axis and the time line on the horizontal axis. Then draw bars to represent the duration of the work package over time. Example 3.8

TIP

If you are asked for a Gantt chart at the start of a project, you could be heading for failure. The Gantt chart is valuable only after you've done the thinking required in Definition, Assign Responsibility, and Sequence Deliverables.

Example 3.8   Gantt Chart

Project Statement

Move the Corporate Customer Services Department within three months at a cost not to exceed $170,000.

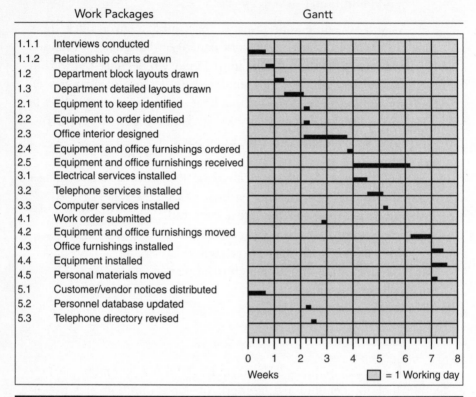

	Work Packages	Gantt
1.1.1	Interviews conducted	
1.1.2	Relationship charts drawn	
1.2	Department block layouts drawn	
1.3	Department detailed layouts drawn	
2.1	Equipment to keep identified	
2.2	Equipment to order identified	
2.3	Office interior designed	
2.4	Equipment and office furnishings ordered	
2.5	Equipment and office furnishings received	
3.1	Electrical services installed	
3.2	Telephone services installed	
3.3	Computer services installed	
4.1	Work order submitted	
4.2	Equipment and office furnishings moved	
4.3	Office furnishings installed	
4.4	Equipment installed	
4.5	Personal materials moved	
5.1	Customer/vendor notices distributed	
5.2	Personnel database updated	
5.3	Telephone directory revised	

Weeks (0 1 2 3 4 5 6 7 8)   ☐ = 1 Working day

depicts a Gantt chart. The solid black lines summarize work package start and end dates.

If you're using project management software to plan your project, you'll be able to highlight the critical path and add the primary person responsible, the names of other resources, and precedence relationships to your Gantt chart. Use the Gantt chart to monitor the performance of the project team and contributors against the deadlines.

Determining the actual dates when work packages will begin and end provides an important basis for communicating progress against the plan. It also informs resources, vendors, suppliers, and contributors when their services will be required on the project and lets stakeholders know the true date the project team is targeting for completion.

PITFALL

Too many work packages scheduled at the same time might be difficult to manage and could also compete for resources. In addition, if more than one is on the critical path, you'll risk delaying the overall deadline.

Join Together

Although it's important to gather scheduling input from resource managers and contributors, creating a first draft on your own will speed up the process. During the next project management activity, Schedule Resources, you'll gain the necessary commitment and acceptance of the schedule.

The More You Know . . .

After scheduling the project work, you may discover the schedule needs to be "crashed." *Crashing* refers to shortening the project schedule by compressing the critical path without changing the sequence of work. It involves a trade-off: shorter work package durations versus potentially higher work package costs, due to adding human or material resources.

Before deciding whether you should crash the schedule, first you must determine if reducing project duration justifies the increased cost and other potential consequences. For example, there may be a penalty associated with project delay greater than the increased cost

PITFALL

You may need to compress the critical path to meet a deadline set by someone else. As you consider ways to compress the critical path (e.g., working overtime, adding resources, splitting into two concurrent work packages), beware of putting too much strain on project resources. Doing this could risk the overall success of the project.

of reducing project duration. Or you may compromise the quality of an output by shortening the duration.

Crashing the critical path won't always result in the time savings you expect. For example:

- Your critical path is 122 days.
- You shave the current critical path by 30 days to 92 days.
- However, your new critical path may be more than 92 days because another path through the project could be longer than 92 days.

You should also take into account what the impact of crashing your project will be on other projects around the organization. Accumulating more resources than you initially planned for might prevent them from being used on other equally important projects, thereby delaying their important deadlines.

To assist you in crashing your schedule, review your project plan and ask the following questions:

- Which work package durations on the critical path can be shortened? How?
- Which work packages can be subdivided to run concurrently?
- How can the relationship or order of work packages on the critical path be altered to shorten the schedule?
- How can slack time be used to complete additional work on the critical path?
- How can slack time be used to reallocate resources to critical path activities?

SCHEDULE RESOURCES

This is the project management activity during which you'll confirm and finalize the scheduling of resources. In Assign Responsibility, you linked work packages with specific individuals and resources. Now you'll ensure these individuals (and their managers) are committed to providing necessary resources (materials, facilities, etc.) and are available for completing their work on scheduled dates.

Your first step in Schedule Resources is to review your project schedule and Responsibility Assignment Matrix. Record the calendar dates associated with each project resource. Include start and finish dates, time-on-task, and slack time for each work package that is the responsibility of the resource. Remember to include individuals who will do the work and also obtain or release other resources (like cash, equipment, storage space, etc.) that you'll need.

Next, revisit the initial work negotiation with each resource manager to reconfirm their commitment of people and materials and to let them know the exact time frame the resources will be needed. If the resource is unavailable at the time you require, consider the following alternatives:

- Alter the schedule to accommodate originally assigned resources if the person or resource is not replaceable. However, it may be possible to use slack time, overtime, and other creative approaches to change the schedule without a significant impact on quality or overall project completion (although they could impact costs). One of the most helpful tools for this is a *resource leveling diagram*. Go to the "Tools: Resource Loading and Leveling" section for more information. (See pages 78–81.)

- Select another resource to perform the function. This may require you to renegotiate with resource managers for another human resource or to settle for a different type of facility, equipment, material, or special resource.

PITFALL

Watch for another difficulty: the cost of obtaining the resource is more than you planned *on the dates when it is needed.* For example, if you need a block of hotel rooms in New York City between the Thanksgiving weekend in late November and New Year's, it will cost significantly more than at most other times.

TIP

If you decide that project contributors must meet a more aggressive schedule, ask them for input. Involving them will help build their commitment to the schedule.

- Outsource the work package to an external resource. While outsourcing may seem like the easy way out of a resource quagmire, remember that outsourcing could boost costs and demand that you closely manage the quality of the work. It can also compromise your ability to develop skills and organizational capability.

After you've scheduled resources for each work package, audit the use of resources in the project plan by asking the following questions:

TIP

Create a project staff directory that includes names, addresses (e-mail and location), phone and fax numbers of all project team members and contributors. Also include any other information the team decides is relevant.

- How many activities is any given resource working on simultaneously? Is this too many?
- On which dates is any given resource not scheduled to do work?
- Are any resources scheduled to work more than 100 percent of their time?

Your answers to these questions might compel you to use *resource loading* or *resource leveling* tools.

Tools: Resource Loading and Leveling

Resource loading and leveling diagrams provide information about resource availability, how the resources are being used, and to what work packages they're assigned.

TIP

Few people work without breaks, interruptions, or distractions. If you've assigned someone to a work package that requires working an eight-hour day, don't be surprised if that work package takes more than a day to complete.

Resource loading diagrams help you allocate resources over the duration of the project. This will ensure you haven't loaded any team members or contributors onto work packages that represent more than 100 percent of their available time. In addition, the diagram will assist you in identifying and capitalizing on those resources that are underutilized. Resource loading diagrams generally require software to construct.

Likewise, a resource leveling diagram will assist you to balance over- and underloading by creating consistent utilization of resources. If you discover that a resource is overloaded, take one of the following actions:

- Extend the duration of the work package to allow more time for the resource to complete it.

- Move resources from other work packages so that it will be completed on time.

- Add resources.

- Shift the work packages around so that the resource can complete it when he or she has time.

Example 3.9 is a before and after picture of a resource's workload. The before diagram shows facilities management skills overloaded for week 8 of the project. The after diagram is a result of decisions that the project manager could make to level the resources. Those decisions might be to: add *lead time* (accelerating the start of a dependent

Example 3.9   Resource Loading and Leveling

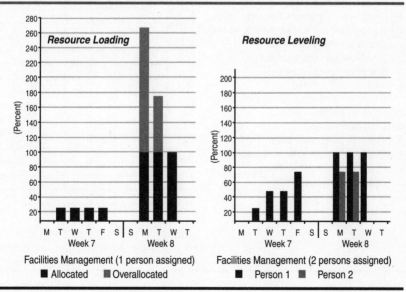

work package) by installing office furnishings (4.3) and equipment (4.4) soon after the start of equipment and office furnishings moved (4.2); use the slack time available in moving personal materials (4.5); and add another resource to those work packages. Lead time can also be added to 4.5 (Personal materials moved). The project manager then updates the resource requirements, responsibility assignment matrix, network diagram, and the Gantt chart (see Example 3.10) to reflect these changes.

Example 3.10   Revised Gantt Chart

Project Statement

Move the Corporate Customer Services Department within three months at a cost not to exceed $170,000.

Work Packages	Gantt

Work Packages	
1.1.1	Interviews conducted
1.1.2	Relationship charts drawn
1.2	Department block layouts drawn
1.3	Department detailed layouts drawn
2.1	Equipment to keep identified
2.2	Equipment to order identified
2.3	Office interior designed
2.4	Equipment and office furnishings ordered
2.5	Equipment and office furnishings received
3.1	Electrical services installed
3.2	Telephone services installed
3.3	Computer services installed
4.1	Work order submitted
4.2	Equipment and office furnishings moved
4.3	Office furnishings installed
4.4	Equipment installed
4.5	Personal materials moved
5.1	Customer/vendor notices distributed
5.2	Personnel database updated
5.3	Telephone directory revised

0   1   2   3   4   5   6   7   8
Weeks   ☐ = 1 Working day
■■■ = Changes to schedule after resource leveling

Most project management software can prepare Resource Loading and Leveling Diagrams. If you have access to a program, use it to develop these diagrams. However, tap your experience and discussions with resource managers to guide decisions about leveling and loading rather than have the program make the decisions for you.

The primary purpose for scheduling resources is to confirm that they will be available when required. Taking care to corroborate dates and times with resource managers and contributors will increase the likelihood of their commitment.

Join Together

At this point in planning your project, you'll need to involve several different groups to help satisfy various needs:

PITFALL

Don't assume that everyone will understand and use your project schedule. Some people may prefer to receive only the dates that affect them. Or they may want to walk through the schedule in a meeting. Probe each group's needs and accommodate them as best you can.

- *Functional managers* (also known as department heads): Depending on your organization, functional managers may be the same people as resource managers, or they may be an entirely different group. If they are different, you should also negotiate with them for the release of their people from other projects and day-to-day work.

- *Senior management* (may also be project sponsors or stakeholders): This is the group that should handle high-level questions regarding priority. Should you remove resources from project A in order to complete project B by the project deadline? Should you increase cost by $30,000 in order to finish the project two weeks early? Prepare well-thought-out alternatives to help senior management make informed decisions.

- *Project team members and contributors:* Tap these groups for input on how to schedule the project more efficiently. They may even have ideas about how to do the work in completely different, more effective ways.

- *Finance department:* Share your plan with them so they can help you manage your cash resources wisely and within company policy.

These groups should also be consulted if you decide to crash the project's critical path. Be prepared to discuss positive and negative consequences, and be sure everyone understands that compressing the critical path can mean higher costs, reduced quality, more risk, and changes to the project scope. Use Potential Problem Analysis (see pages 83–87) to prepare for potential problems that crashing the critical path might cause.

The More You Know . . .

As project manager, you may be held accountable to organizational standards for cash expenditures. If this is the case, you'll probably want to scrutinize how and when cash needs to be spent during the project. You can do this by creating a *spend plan*—a report of when you'll spend cash to acquire resources, when you'll actually use those resources, and for how long you'll need the resources.

A spend plan addresses these aspects because they can lead to additional costs. Take, for example, the cost implications of acquiring materials that aren't needed until months later. You may incur additional costs such as warehousing and transportation.

Your spend plan will help you balance costs over the span of the project, forecasting when you're going to need cash resources and how much you'll need. It can also help prevent you from exceeding the spend limit for any given time period.

PROTECT AND ENHANCE THE PLAN

The project statement is written, the objectives are developed, and the WBS has been fleshed out. The work packages are sequenced and scheduled. The resources are assigned and scheduled. Your project plan is finished, right?

Wrong. One of the most important yet overlooked facets of successful project management is the ability to identify—and prepare for—things that could go wrong. In "Protect the Plan," you'll identify where problems might occur, which problems concern you the most, and what actions you'll take to prevent or contain them.

Tool: Potential Problem Analysis

How do you sort through the hundreds, perhaps thousands, of negative scenarios that could develop during the course of your project? And once they are identified how do you stop them from negatively impacting your project plan?

Dr. Charles Kepner and Dr. Benjamin Tregoe developed a technique in the late 1950s called *Potential Problem Analysis* (PPA). It is a step-by-step method for identifying what could go wrong when undertaking a project and actually planning actions for prevention and containment.

PPA requires six steps that can be as detailed or as cursory as you wish:

1. Identify areas in the plan where you anticipate problems or where problems could most severely impact success.

2. Identify the specific problems that could occur.

3. List the likely causes for these problems.

4. Plan actions that will prevent the likely causes from occurring.

5. Plan actions that will minimize the impact if the problems do occur.

6. Modify your project plan to include those actions.

To complete step 1 (identify areas of the plan where you anticipate problems), have

PITFALL

Your project team members or contributors might label PPA as "pessimistic" or a "waste of time." If this occurs, try these explanations: (1) PPA is actually proactive because it seeks to remove problems from the future and (2) if you have the time to go back and fix things when they go wrong, you have time to prevent them now.

your project plan available and ask the following questions about the work packages:

- Where do you anticipate problems?
- Where will problems impact the plan most in terms of time, cost, and performance? Which ones are on the critical path?
- Where is work most complex?
- Where will something new be attempted?
- Where will new employees be involved?
- Where have you failed before?
- Where is responsibility shared or unclear?

Use your answers to target the work packages you'll analyze. Then identify specific problems that could occur (step 2) in each work package. When thinking of what could go wrong, consider how the following could impact the successful completion of a work package:

- Natural phenomena (like flooding, earthquakes, blizzards)
- Work setting of the project team or contributors
- Expectations, misunderstood goals, or pressure from others
- Incorrect information
- Poor estimates
- Poorly skilled staff
- Completing the action itself
- Design errors, changes in requirements, resourcing shortages, scheduling conflicts

Construct a table with five columns and enter your potential problems into the first column. Refer to Example 3.11.

Next, consider the probability and seriousness of each potential problem, one at a time, and identify those you'll attempt to prevent. Choose potential problems that will have a serious impact on your plan in terms of meeting key objectives, satisfying customers,

Example 3.11   Protect the Plan

Critical area of the plan: 3.3 Computer services installed.

Potential Problem	Likely Causes	Preventive Actions	Contingent Actions	Triggers
Users can't access their network files after the move.	Likely Cause #1: Improper packing of the server causes damage during the move.	Assign technical staff to be on site throughout the move to monitor packing.	Recheck Internet Protocol (IP) addresses and hub connections.	A user calls technical staff and reports he can't retrieve files.
		Check packing and positioning before server is moved.	Install backup mirror server.	Jerry Harper reads error messages upon server boot up.
	Likely Cause #2: Lightning damages power supply.	Accept the risk; no action will be taken.		
	Likely Cause #3: Data cable is not installed properly.	Test cable before connecting workstations.		
		Install all network connections between data outlets and computers.		
		Provide technicians with accurate documentation for hub connections.		

Modify the plan

Add the following actions to the project plan:

    Check packing and positioning before server is moved.

    Test cable before connecting workstations.

    Inspect all network connections between data outlets and computers.

    Give technicians accurate documentation for hub connections.

    Assign responsibility to recheck Internet Protocol (IP) addresses and hub connections.

    Prepare backup so ready if needed.

    Install backup mirror server.

    Copy server data to backup mirror server.

    Send e-mail to tell users to call us if they can't access the network.

TIP

When writing likely causes, make sure you include what is likely to cause the problem and how it will cause the problem. Doing so will point to how you can prevent the problem. For example, one likely cause of a factory fire could be that solvents are not stored correctly. Storing them properly in the future could prevent another fire.

conserving resources, ensuring safety, and are very likely to happen if you don't take action. Don't waste time and money preparing for trivial problems. For the serious and highly probable ones, ask yourself and your team, "What could cause this potential problem to occur?" Your answers are *likely causes*. Enter them into the second column of your table (step 3). As Example 3.11 shows, there may be more than one likely cause for each potential problem.

Consider each likely cause one at a time. In the third column of your table list *preventive actions* (step 4)—actions taken to prevent each likely cause. For example, if you identify a potential problem as "Installation of e-mail application delayed" and a likely cause as "Our information technology department lacks the skills required to install the application," one preventive action could be "Send two information technology department employees to training prior to start of installation project." As Example 3.11 shows, there may be more than one preventive action for each likely cause.

Finally, redirect your attention to the potential problems. What if this potential problem occurred despite your efforts to prevent it? What would you do to minimize the damage? Your answers to these questions become *contingent actions* (step 5)—actions you'll prepare now but will only use if the potential problem occurs. As Example 3.11 shows, there may be more than one contingent action for each potential problem.

TIP

When adding preventive and contingent actions to your plan, you will need to go back and refine the WBS, the resource requirements, the RAM, the network diagram, and the Gantt chart. You may also elect not to plan for some of these actions because of the impact on your budget.

Record contingent actions in the fourth column of the table and make sure you add a *trigger* (part of step 5) for each one in the fifth column. A trigger warns you the potential problem has occurred, and, if necessary, initiates the contingent action. For example, if you are launching a new foot powder product, and you identify your potential problem as "Allergic reaction by customers causes negative product publicity," one contingent action might be "Submit test results to the media, demonstrating product safety." Your trigger might be "100 customers call our customer service line to report allergic reaction" or "Media representative calls us for our comment on allergic reaction to the product."

It is also possible to have several triggers for the same potential problem. In this case, each trigger would start different contingent actions, depending on the actual timing and severity of the problem. For example, being two days behind schedule three weeks into the project might trigger a different response than being one week behind schedule with only one week prior to the scheduled finish date.

TIP

Specificity is essential when thinking about the damage that could be caused by a potential problem. Being specific will allow you to focus on the most appropriate contingent action to take. Ask, "If this [potential problem] occurs, what is likely to happen?" Record your answers as a list of *likely effects*, and then set contingent action(s) for each likely effect. Doing this will give you a greater number of actions you can prepare for should the potential problem occur.

The final step of PPA is just as important as the previous five—transforming your thinking into action. Modify your project plan (step 6) by adding preventive actions, contingent actions, and triggers as work packages. Treat them as you would any other work package, including the primary resources responsible, a start and finish date, and performance expectations. If necessary, change the WBS and resource requirements to reflect the additional work. If this increases the overall budget, it must be justified in terms of reduced risk and agreed to by the customer and/or stakeholders.

Preventing problems, and being ready to fight them if they do occur, gives you a better chance to complete your project on time, within budget, and with acceptable performance.

PITFALL

Once the danger of the potential problem has passed, remove the preparations you've made for the contingent action. Keeping these actions in place when they are no longer required may lead to unnecessary cost or additional problems.

Join Together

The two most valuable groups of people to involve in protecting your plan against risk and adverse consequences are (1) those who have managed or contributed to similar projects in the past and (2) those who are completely new to this type of project. Experienced individuals bring a well-honed knowledge of the "usual suspects"—those problems that seem to happen every time. Novices supply a fresh perspective. Their thinking is not hindered by ideas of "the way things should be" or "this is what always happens."

The More You Know . . .

It's not always necessary to conduct a full PPA, carefully carrying out and documenting all six steps. Depending on the nature of your project, you can use a full PPA (complex, high-impact projects) or short-version PPA thinking (simple, less important projects). Use enough PPA to reduce project risks to acceptable levels. Depending on the consequences of late completion, or even complete project failure, more analysis and preventive and contingent actions may be needed.

For a short-version of PPA, ask questions like:

- What could go wrong?
- What would cause it to go wrong?
- What can I do to stop it from going wrong?
- What will I do if it does go wrong?

Thinking about the answers (and what you can do to prepare) will help protect the action you're about to take. For example, when driving to the airport you could get a flat tire, run out of gas, get caught in traffic, and so on. How you prevent and prepare for these events could mean the difference between catching your flight in time or missing it.

A quick PPA can also be useful as you move from Planning into Implementation, especially if a change outside your control comes to your attention. For example, you suddenly learn that a key employee will be absent for three days. By quickly jotting down potential problems, you may find that actions like immediate reallocation of key people are necessary.

You may feel there's not enough good information to do a PPA. However, keep in mind you're constantly taking what you have learned in the past to predict the future. Similarly, you can upgrade information for use in a PPA if you:

- Ask specific questions. Too often the issues you're trying to predict are global. By separating and making questions specific, the issues not only become easier to handle, but also suggest available information that will help.

- Look at basic cause-and-effect relationships that influence the outcome you're trying to predict; get available information about these factors. Past records and projected changes can then be assessed to make more accurate judgments.

There's always the temptation to include contingency funds in the budget to deal with problems that you didn't anticipate. This can be effective, but only if you have a good understanding of the reasons for doing so. For example, some organizations tack on a standard percentage of the project budget for contingencies (such as 10 percent or 15 percent), no matter what the project. However, what happens when it comes time to allocate contingency funds? How will you know how much to allocate, given that there may be overruns further along in the project? By assessing risks for each work package and calculating a contingency amount based on this analysis, you'll have a better idea of how much total contingency money you'll need and how much can be allocated for each potential problem. If there's an early need for project funds in an area you identified as low risk, you'll know you have to be cautious in your expenditure.

ENHANCE THE PLAN

After looking into the future to determine what could go wrong, step back and put on your thinking cap. Consider things that could go better than expected. The types of things you're looking for include:

- Ways the plan could be completed even more effectively.
- Ways the plan could be completed at less cost.

- Additional organizational benefits that could result from doing the project or some of the work packages.

- Places where just a small improvement in time, money, or performance could yield large benefits.

Tool: Potential Opportunity Analysis

Potential Opportunity Analysis (POA), the tool for encouraging things to go even better than expected and capitalizing on them when they do, uses logic similar to that of PPA. You examine the plan for areas where there's the possibility for large benefit, identify the potential opportunities and likely causes, and record actions to promote them. Then, reexamining the potential opportunities, you prepare for actions that will capitalize on them if they do happen and add triggers to alert you that the opportunity is about to occur.

Construct a five-column table similar to PPA, keeping in mind that the results of your POA should also become part of the project plan. Example 3.12 on page 91 shows a POA for work package 2.5 Equipment and office furnishings received.

ADDITIONAL PLANNING TOPICS

More about Critical Path

Think of the critical path as a jigsaw puzzle composed of many pieces of unequal length. As one puzzle piece ends, the next one (which is dependent on its predecessor) begins. Fit the pieces together and they reveal a picture.

The puzzle pieces are your work packages—some are longer than others, but each one depends on its predecessor. Ideally, as each work package ends on time, the next one begins on time, and so on throughout the project. The cumulation of work package durations on the critical path is the total duration for the project.

There is more than one method for calculating the critical path and communicating it to your project team. Use the *forward and backward pass* to calculate the critical path. Review Example 3.13 on

Example 3.12   Enhance the Plan

Critical area of the plan: 2.5 Equipment and office furnishings received.

Potential Opportunity	Likely Cause	Promoting Actions	Capitalizing Actions	Triggers
Equipment and furnishings arrive earlier than expected.	Vendor expedites order.	Call vendor with pre-order information.	Complete office preparations earlier in the schedule.	Vendor confirms earlier date with Facilities manager.
		Offer to expedite payment.	Ace Movers start move earlier.	Facilities manager calls Ace Movers the next day.

Modify the plan

Add the following actions to the project plan:

Contact vendor about expediting equipment and office furnishings order. If successful, notify Receiving.

Accounting to expedite vendor payment.

Reschedule the move and installation of equipment and office furnishings work packages for completion earlier.

Contact Ace Movers to arrange for possible earlier move.

---

pages 92 and 93. This table shows the work packages, their duration, and the earliest and latest start and finish times. To calculate the earliest start and finish times using the forward pass, do the following:

- Assume that each work package begins immediately after the related preceding work package is completed.

- Determine the earliest finish time using a simple formula:

    Earliest start time + Duration = Earliest finish time

- Begin at the start node of your project and make a forward pass through the project plan by determining the earliest point in time each work package can begin and end.

- Start at zero. The earliest start time for the work package that begins at the first node is zero.

Example 3.13 Critical Path Method

Project Statement

Move the Corporate Customer Services department within three months at a cost not to exceed $170,000.

Work Packages	Precedence	Duration (Days)	Earliest Start	Earliest Finish	Latest Start	Latest Finish	Slack (Days)	Critical Path
S—Start of project			0	0	0	0	0	Yes
1.1.1 Interviews conducted	None	3	0	3	0	3	0	Yes
1.1.2 Relationship charts drawn	1.1.1	2	3	5	3	5	0	Yes
1.2 Department block layouts drawn	1.1.2	2	5	7	5	7	0	Yes
1.3 Department detailed layouts drawn	1.2	4	7	11	7	11	0	Yes
2.1 Equipment to keep identified	1.3	1	11	12	18	19	7	
2.2 Equipment to order identified	1.3	1	11	12	18	19	7	
2.3 Office interior designed	1.3	8	11	19	11	19	0	Yes
2.4 Equipment and office furnishings ordered	2.1, 2.2, 2.3	1	19	20	19	20	0	Yes
2.5 Equipment and office furnishings received	2.4	11	20	31	20	31	0	Yes
3.1 Electrical services installed	1.3	3	11	14	28	31	17	
3.2 Telephone services installed	1.3	3	11	14	28	31	17	
3.3 Computer services installed	1.3	1	11	12	30	31	19	

Task	Predecessor							
4.1 Work order submitted	1.3	1	11	12	30	31	19	
4.2 Equipment/office furnishings moved	2.5, 3.1, 3.2, 3.3, 4.1	4	31	35	31	35	0	Yes
4.3 Office furnishings installed	4.2	2	35	37	36	38	1	
4.4 Equipment installed	4.2	3	35	38	35	38	0	Yes
4.5 Personal materials moved	4.2	1	35	36	37	38	2	
5.1 Customer/vendor notices distributed	None	4	0	4	34	38	34	
5.2 Personnel database updated	1.3	1	11	12	37	38	26	
5.3 Telephone directory revised	1.3	1	11	12	37	38	26	
F—Project finished	4.4	0	38	38	38	38	0	Yes

Next, calculate the latest finish time and latest start time for each work package using the *backward pass*. Follow these steps:

- Determine the latest start time using a simple formula:

    Latest finish − Duration = Latest start time

- Begin at the finish node, using the earliest finish time of the last work package as the starting point. Then, make a backward pass through the project plan by determining the latest time each work package can begin and end and still complete the project by the earliest finish time.

Now compare the earliest finish and latest finish times. If they are not the same, then that work package has slack time and is off the critical path. You can also use this formula:

    Latest start [or finish] time − Earliest start [or finish] time = Slack time

Once again, review Example 3.13. Work packages 1.1.1, 1.1.2, and 1.2 (among others) do not have slack time and therefore are on the critical path. The path through the project network that determines the shortest time within which the project can be completed (zero slack time for all tasks on that path) is the critical path. Example 3.13 displays a table that includes a column labeled "Critical Path." Check that column to see which work packages are on the critical path.

More about Program Evaluation and Review Technique

Program Evaluation and Review Technique (PERT) uses a statistical approach to arrive at the project's duration. PERT is a variation of the critical path method. Like the critical path method, it is developed along network diagram principles. The critical path method, however, bases its time estimates on historical data, and work package durations are generally the average time that it has taken to complete similar work packages in the past. Sometimes, though, you will not have historical data to go by and you will have to rely on experience and good judgment to figure out how long it's going to take you to complete the work packages. PERT approximates the average completion time, thereby giving you a better understanding of when your work packages will probably be completed.

PERT relies on the weighted average of three time estimates—optimistic, most likely, and pessimistic—to determine the expected completion time for each work package (see Example 3.14). You can then calculate the critical path and the completion times for the project. This technique is used when work packages contain a high degree of uncertainty. For example, if a supplier can deliver a hard-to-obtain resource on time, you could finish a particular work package within a few weeks, but if the supplier cannot deliver the resource for several months, then your project's time line could change significantly. It is also a useful technique to use when you are undertaking a unique project, one that has a great deal of risk, where the results are difficult to predict—such as a research and development project—and where there is no historical information to guide you. A PERT calculation will give you a better understanding of duration probabilities and the duration boundaries within which you can complete the project.

To calculate PERT:

- Assign three time estimates to every work package.
- Determine the weighted average for each work package using this formula:

$$\frac{(1 \times \text{Optimistic}) + (4 \times \text{Most likely}) + (1 \times \text{Pessimistic})}{6}$$

- Calculate the project's duration using the forward and backward pass, as you did in the critical path method.

Example 3.14   Calculating PERT

Project Statement

Move the Corporate Customer Services department within three months at a cost not to exceed $170,000.

Work Packages	Duration	Optimistic Duration	Most Likely Duration	Pessimistic Duration
1.1.1 Interviews conducted	3d	1d	3d	5d
1.1.2 Relationship charts drawn	2.17d	1d	2d	4d
1.2 Department block layouts drawn	2d	1d	2d	3d
1.3 Department detailed layouts drawn	4.33d	3d	4d	7d
2.1 Equipment to keep identified	2.17d	1d	2d	4d
2.2 Equipment to order identified	2d	1d	2d	3d
2.3 Office interior designed	8.83d	6d	8d	15d
2.4 Equipment and office furnishings ordered	2d	1d	2d	3d
2.5 Equipment and office furnishings received	11.5d	5d	11d	20d

PLANNING SUMMARY

It was Lady MacBeth who warned, "What's done cannot be undone."

Perhaps this is an exaggerated statement. Perhaps not. Regardless, in Planning you map out exactly who is going to do what, when they are going to do it in calendar time, and how you're going to mitigate risks. This lays the groundwork for producing results during Implementation.

chapter
4

project
implementation

THE PLAN IS NOW in hand, and the project team members review it one last time. They reveal additional potential problems and add preventive and contingent actions to the plan. They are now ready to get to work.

The project starts smoothly, in part due to Tim Dwight's (remember, Tim is the project manager) experience. During Planning, he focused part of the Potential Problem Analysis (PPA) on the start-up activities. However, the team faces a slew of conflicts as implementation continues. The facilities manager submits her resignation to the company, so the team loses a critical resource. Vice President of Corporate Customer Services Peter Baldwin, who is responsible for the project funds, intends to keep an eagle eye fixed on each piece of the project to make sure the budget is adhered to. Other personnel changes and scope changes pop up, and the team is forced to alter the plan along the way.

ARE YOU READY TO DO THE WORK?

After defining the reasons for doing the project and planning how it will be accomplished, you should be ready to move into Implementation. This is where "sweating the Definition and Planning" helps you minimize "bleeding the Implementation." It's now time to do the work.

Guided by the project plan, you'll use project resources to produce the deliverables that will fulfill the project statement and objectives.

During Implementation, you and your project team will answer five questions:

1. How will work start?

2. How will the project team and contributors communicate during implementation, and what kinds of documentation will they be expected to produce?

3. How will the project be monitored and how should progress be reported?

4. How will concerns (uncovered during monitoring) impact the project plan?

5. What activities will be completed to evaluate and finalize the project?

Four Implementation activities will assist you in answering these questions:

1. Start to Implement

2. Monitor the Project

3. Modify the Project

4. Closeout and Evaluate

Before you start to implement, "freeze" your project plan so that you can compare the original to the final, changed plan. The original establishes a baseline and allows you to track how the project is actually doing against the plan. Some software packages will automate baselining for you.

START TO IMPLEMENT

Implementation can start several weeks, or even months, after you've defined and planned the project. This gap, however small, will probably require you to review and revisit some of the resource commitments gained during the previous planning activities.

Review the plan and pay special attention to the initial days and weeks of the project. A project that starts with a stumble tends to finish badly. Confirm that your project team and contributors know when their time or resources are needed and, just as important, when their project activities should begin.

TIP

Reserve a conference room or office space (sometimes called a "war room") where project artifacts like schedules and records can be kept and maintained. You and your team can also use this space to conduct impromptu project meetings and store shared project documentation. Make schedules and issue resolution visible on the walls.

It's also critical that everyone involved understand the project statement and objectives. If you haven't done so already, provide your project team and contributors with the specific "why" behind their work, as well as how their activities relate to overall project goals.

In addition, meet with your project team to establish *ground rules*. Ground rules are operating principles that govern a project team as they implement the project plan. They can be as trivial as, "Team members can call each other at home before 10 P.M. during the work week, and between 11 A.M. and 11 P.M. on weekends"; or as critical as, "Each team member must submit a status report using the designated template every Friday before 3 P.M." (See Example 4.1.)

Ground rules should address three main areas:

1. Working together
2. Controlling changes in the project and work environment
3. Improving project monitoring

Let's look at these in more detail.

Example 4.1   Ground Rules

Subject: Ground Rules   August 9
To: Corporate Customer Services Project Team
From: Tim Dwight

Thanks for participating in yesterday's kickoff meeting. As discussed, along with the project baseline, please keep the following ground rules available for easy reference throughout the project.

- Don't hesitate to come to me, but look first to the person with primary responsibility for your tasks if you have questions or concerns about your work.
- Please seek out approval for any overtime of more than two hours or unbudgeted expenses of more than $250.
- This project will be moving fast. Please report the following to me:
  —One day prior to your task's date, confirm your readiness.
  —Once a day while the task is underway, report percent complete and concerns.
  —On the day of completion, confirm with Actual versus Plan for time and cost, and any remaining concerns.
- Use e-mail for routine reporting.
- Use the phone and voice mail for any urgent issues.
- It is okay to call me at home after hours and during the weekend.

I look forward to our working together and seeing us all comfortably ensconced in our spanking new offices.

Any project team that wants to succeed needs clear, accepted principles for *working together*. To do this, establish:

- The decision-making authority of each member of the project team (e.g., Who will be responsible for making changes to the project plan?)

- How conflicts with the customer, the organization, and other contributors should be resolved (e.g., Should they be immediately escalated to the project manager or handled by each team member?)

- How feedback on individual performance will be communicated (e.g., in a monthly report or informally by the project manager as work is completed?)

- How new ideas and suggestions will be handled (e.g., Should they be included in a weekly status report or sent immediately to the project manager?)

- How team members will communicate among themselves (e.g., Is e-mail the preferred method? What information should be handled over the phone and what should be saved for project meetings?)

- How project status and customer feedback will be reported to the team (e.g., Will you hold bi-weekly face-to-face meetings, or will you put out a daily e-mail, or both?).

An established method for handling and controlling changes is also paramount to the success of the project. To do this, you and your project team will agree on:

- How problems and potential problems will be reported (e.g., What magnitude of cost or schedule overrun warrants an immediate alert to the project manager?)

- How changes to the project plan will be documented and communicated (e.g., Will a new project plan be sent to the team each time a change is made? What changes require written approval from the customer?)

- Who possesses the authority to approve changes (e.g., Who else besides the project manager can approve a change to resources, schedule, and/or deliverables?)

A third aspect to consider when crafting ground rules is improving *project monitoring*. These guidelines will set the groundwork for the later activity, Modify the Project. They include determining:

- What information should be reported back to the project manager, how often, and in what format (e.g., weekly status reports).

Checklist 4.1   Helping You Start to Implement

Starting out your project on the right note is critical to a successful outcome. The checklist topics listed below can help steer you away from some of the usual communication breakdowns that are often part of a project launch.

Checklist

- √ Individual and/or group communications planned
- √ Project documentation assembled to guide implementation
- √ Materials, facilities, equipment, funding, and so on in place for initial tasks
- √ Ground rules established for team interaction, communication
- √ Potential Problem Analysis and Potential Opportunity Analysis done for critical initial tasks
- √ Team and team member performance expectations agreed to and in place
- √ Monitoring systems and methods agreed to and in place
- √ Issue-resolution protocols agreed to and in place
- √ Reporting systems and methods agreed to and in place
- √ Change-control systems agreed to and in place

- How the project team will record their time and expenses (e.g., Have you established a project code and codes within it to match major deliverables?).

In the Corporate Customer Services example, Tim Dwight holds a kickoff meeting. Since avoiding a disruption in customer service during the office move is crucial, everyone who will be involved in the project is invited. The project plan and responsibility assignments are reviewed and questions from the group are discussed. The meeting is short but beneficial. The discussion clears up questions about moving the computer, plans for the new office space, equipment being purchased, time frame for the actual move, and so on. Also discussed are reporting responsibilities, review meetings, escalation of issues, potential problems and opportunities, and so on. As a result of

Example 4.2   Project Baseline Schedule

Project Statement

Move the Corporate Customer Services Department within three months at a cost not to exceed $170,000.

Work Packages   Gantt

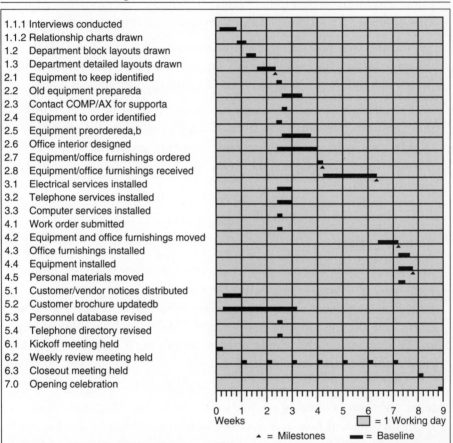

1.1.1	Interviews conducted
1.1.2	Relationship charts drawn
1.2	Department block layouts drawn
1.3	Department detailed layouts drawn
2.1	Equipment to keep identified
2.2	Old equipment prepareda
2.3	Contact COMP/AX for supporta
2.4	Equipment to order identified
2.5	Equipment preordereda,b
2.6	Office interior designed
2.7	Equipment/office furnishings ordered
2.8	Equipment/office furnishings received
3.1	Electrical services installed
3.2	Telephone services installed
3.3	Computer services installed
4.1	Work order submitted
4.2	Equipment and office furnishings moved
4.3	Office furnishings installed
4.4	Equipment installed
4.5	Personal materials moved
5.1	Customer/vendor notices distributed
5.2	Customer brochure updatedb
5.3	Personnel database revised
5.4	Telephone directory revised
6.1	Kickoff meeting held
6.2	Weekly review meeting held
6.3	Closeout meeting held
7.0	Opening celebration

0   1   2   3   4   5   6   7   8   9
Weeks   □ = 1 Working day
▲ = Milestones   ▬ = Baseline

[a] Potential problem analysis revisions.
[b] Potential opportunity analysis revisions.

the discussions, the plans changed slightly, and this is reflected in the Gantt chart in Example 4.2 on page 105. The overall budget was baselined at $165,483 and the overall duration at 45 days, an increase of 7 days from the initial 38 days. Review meetings were scheduled for Monday of each week. A closeout meeting and opening celebration were added to the Gantt chart as well as new work packages resulting from Potential Problem and Opportunity Analyses.

You and your project team should use the checklist on page 104 as thought-starters for establishing your own set of ground rules. Your list should reflect the unique needs of your organization and project.

Preparing to start may seem like overkill after all the planning that you have just done but, in fact, taking the time to do this thoroughly can help prevent common start-up problems, especially if some time has elapsed between the project planning and the start-up.

Join Together

The theme throughout this activity is communication with your project team and contributors—reconfirming expectations and commitments, revisiting the project statement and objectives, and developing ground rules. This does not always require face-to-face meetings. Depending on the number and proximity of team members, it may be easier to send a quick e-mail or voice mail.

At the same time, don't ignore the benefit of bringing the project team together. Gathering people in one place (at one time) ensures that everyone will hear the same message. In addition, it creates the opportunity for participants to get to know one another more personally, propose ideas to the entire group, or resolve pre-implementation concerns. It may also provide an opportunity for the project sponsor or for a senior manager or champion to address the team and show his or her support for the project.

If you're having trouble deciding whether to hold a face-to-face meeting, first establish meeting objectives. Do you want the people involved to interact individually? Do you merely want information from each of the members? Do you need to dig further into concerns?

Then ask yourself, "Is there another way to meet these objectives besides a face-to-face meeting?" For more on running project meetings, see Meetings and Communication on page 164.

The More You Know . . .

If your project requires a formal start, schedule a kickoff meeting for project team members and contributors. This will give you the opportunity to socialize your project plan, review commitments, and officially initiate the project, while providing them with the chance to ask questions and clarify potential misunderstandings.

MONITOR THE PROJECT

Your project has now begun, and you are consuming resources and producing deliverables—hopefully not without a watchful eye. In this activity, you'll tackle project monitoring—watching how your project is operating compared to what you planned.

Put simply, monitoring asks you to make decisions regarding *what* will be monitored and *when* it will be monitored. And, if you haven't done so already, you'll determine *how* this data will be reported and *who* will receive the report.

TIP

Save project reports. Not only are they important during project implementation, but they also contribute to a project history that you and others can review and learn from in the future.

You should ensure that *all* time, cost, and performance data are gathered from *all* work packages; this will present a picture of the overall project. However, as project manager, you'll have neither the time nor the energy to review in detail this tonnage of data. Instead, you must decide how to best allocate your time and attention to this data. *This is the act of monitoring.*

So, what will you monitor? Examine the three areas described next—time, cost, and performance—for guidance on how to monitor.

Time

Most project managers choose to monitor the project's critical path, since it determines whether the project will ultimately be completed on time. However, there are other aspects you can focus your attention on, including:

- Delay of work packages not on the critical path
- Work packages completed ahead of schedule
- Lag time needed versus lag time planned
- Triggers or thresholds

Above all, what you choose to monitor should alert you if the project has fallen behind or is ahead of schedule. Example 4.3 shows duration variances for completed work packages. Work package 2.6 Office interior designed, which was originally eight days long, now shows a duration of 16 days, but the overall duration increase for major deliverable 2. Office Equipment is only two days. This was accomplished through the judicious use of lead and slack time.

Cost

Keeping a project within budget can be a tough battle. Your best chance for success starts with realistic estimates and a strong commitment to monitoring resource expenditures. Calculate how much of your budgeted resources you've spent (this can include cash, materials, people hours, etc.) compared to the budget for the work completed, and how much remains to complete the project. Example 4.4 on page 110 contains a column that charts the cost variance—the difference between planned cost and actual cost—for each work package. It shows several work packages being over the budget limit, indicating that major deliverable 2. Office Equipment is close to $6,870 over its baseline cost. These costs were incurred partly through the acquisition of additional equipment and because of underestimating interior designer involvement.

Performance

In Definition, you established objectives to identify project goals. You also may have constructed a WBS dictionary and populated it

Example 4.3 Time Variance

Work Packages	Baseline Duration (Days)	Actual Duration (Days)	Duration Variance (Days)	Baseline Start	Actual Start	Baseline Finish	Actual Finish
2.0 Office equipment	20	22	2	7/24	7/22	8/20	8/20
2.1 Equipment to keep identified	1	2	1	7/24	7/25	7/24	7/26
2.2 Old equipment prepared	3	3	0	7/25	7/29	7/29	7/31
2.3 Contact COMP/AX for support	1	1	0	7/25	7/29	7/25	7/29
2.4 Equipment to order identified	1	2	1	7/24	7/25	7/24	7/26
2.5 Equipment preordered	5	5	0	7/25	7/29	7/31	8/2
2.6 Office interior designed	8	16	8	7/24	7/22	8/2	8/12
2.7 Equipment/office furnishings ordered	1	8	7	8/5	8/5	8/5	8/14
2.8 Equipment/office furnishings received	11	10	−1	8/6	8/6	8/20	8/20

Example 4.4   Cost Variance

Work Packages	Baseline Cost ($)	Actual Cost ($)	Cost Variance ($)
2.0 Office equipment	78,947.87	85,816.98	6,869.12
2.1 Equipment to keep identified	960.37	1,920.00	74,960.36
2.2 Old equipment prepared	2,000.00	1,654.00	(346.00)
2.3 Contact COMP/AX for support	0.00	0.00	0.00
2.4 Equipment to order identified	937.50	1,875.00	937.50
2.5 Equipment preordered	0.00	0.00	0.00
2.6 Office interior designed	5,050.00	7,367.25	2,317.25
2.7 Equipment/office furnishings ordered	70,000.00	73,000.00	3,000.00
2.8 Equipment/office furnishings received	0.00	0.00	0.00

with performance standards. These objectives and performance expectations now become the primary sources for monitoring project performance.

To monitor project performance against goals, ask:

- What will tell us if we are meeting the objectives?
- How well is our performance meeting the objectives?

Answering these questions will require that you and your project team engage in *predictive monitoring*. Predictive monitoring involves judging whether project objectives will be met by the end of the project . . . based on progress made against them to date. If some of your objectives will be met several months or years later, there's even more reason to monitor progress now so that you'll have a factual basis for judging whether the objective will eventually be met. If you determine that objectives might not be fulfilled, you'll take action in the next activity—Modify the Project.

There are many approaches to "when" you should monitor a project. Some project managers prefer to scrutinize the start and finish of every work package; others monitor at a weekly or monthly interval. Still others only pay attention to certain work packages on the critical path. How often you choose to monitor will depend on the size and complexity of your project, as well as your personal style of managing. At a minimum, compare the plan to the actual work being completed to see how the project is doing.

See Example 4.5 for a snapshot of how work is progressing during implementation of the Corporate Customer Services project. You will find that the work for major deliverable 2.

PITFALL

Don't provide every project detail to customers and stakeholders—it invites them to resolve minor concerns that are better left to the project manager and team. However, don't hide facts or significant threats to the project from them.

Office equipment has increased by almost 79 hours over the original estimate of 141 hours. This was caused by internal workstation returns being delayed in shipment and by the change in facilities management leadership.

It's possible that you'll need to monitor some parts of the project plan more frequently than others. For example, you may monitor the project after every work package along the critical path to ensure that the project is on schedule but reserve the rest of your monitoring for milestones (see "Walking the Milestones" on page 112). To determine how often you should monitor the project, answer the following questions:

Example 4.5 Work Variance

Work Packages	Baseline Work (Hours)	Actual Work (Hours)	Work Variance (Hours)
2.0 Office equipment	140.4	218.55	78.15
2.1 Equipment to keep identified	14	28	14
2.2 Old equipment prepared	24	24	0
2.3 Contact COMP/AX for support	2	2	0
2.4 Equipment to order identified	15	30	15
2.5 Equipment preordered	12	12	0
2.6 Office interior designed	43	86	43
2.7 Equipment/office furnishings ordered	10	32	22
2.8 Equipment/office furnishings received	5	4.55	−0.45

Walking the Milestones

One approach to monitoring is the use of *milestones*. Milestones are specific points in the project plan that correspond with the completion of major components of the project, such as an important major deliverable, a project phase, a work package, or a subproject. Technically speaking, milestones are events of zero duration and don't consume resources. They represent the instant at which something is started or completed. However, milestone activities like scheduled reviews will consume resources and need to be planned.

Use project milestones to mark the points in time to monitor critical portions of the project. Conduct review meetings around project milestones.

Choosing when to place milestones in the project schedule is key to successfully monitoring your project. Create scenarios that represent where you'll set milestones. Here's a list of some points to consider:

- When important decisions will be made
- When work packages that affect project timing will be started or completed (for example, work packages on the critical path)
- When major deliverables that have a significant impact on cost will be started or completed
- When major deliverables that affect key project objectives are started or completed
- When an historically difficult work package will be started or completed
- When something will be tested that may affect project success
- The start or completion of a subproject

As the project reaches a milestone, you'll monitor the schedule, cost, and performance. The triangles shown in Example 4.2 represent milestones for the Corporate Customer Services project.

- When will periodic monitoring provide sufficient information to manage results?
- When will detailed, frequent monitoring improve project performance?

Monitor the Project is closely tied to Modify the Project, the next Implementation activity. As you and your project team monitor time, cost, and performance, you'll uncover a variety of *concerns*. In Modify the Project, you'll analyze these concerns and determine how the project will need to be changed to accommodate them.

Allowing your project plan to proceed without monitoring can be a disaster. If you're extremely lucky, all work packages will be completed on time, within budget, and with the desired results. But don't count on it. Instead, construct a system for monitoring the project so you can measure actual progress against the plan and thus increase your chances for success.

You can report monitoring results in two different ways. You can use a formal reporting method, sending out a project report on a periodic basis. Or you can engage in informal conversations with your project participants. The best approach is a combination of the two; use the formal reporting cycle to publicize project progress and informal reporting to provide essential, real-time data.

Your project team could require more instructions on reporting than you provided in the Start to Implement activity. For example, project stakeholders may ask you for monitoring results every month or after every milestone. In addition, they might expect to receive results in a certain format. If this is the case, prepare report templates for your project team. Here are some of the types of reports you can create:

PITFALL

In the absence of feedback, people will draw their own conclusions about the quality of their work. Make sure you feed back information to team members and project contributors (gathered during monitoring) based on their performance to date.

PITFALL

Don't overlook concerns that are identified outside the bounds of your project monitoring. Stakeholders, management, and others may raise concerns about the value or progress of the project. If you don't address their issues, you'll risk alienating them, or even worse, ignoring a concern that negatively impacts your project.

- Spend plan versus actual spending
- Work plan versus actual
- Planned commitments versus actual
- Cost, schedule, or performance by account, work order, or performer
- Costs by cost center
- Potential problems and opportunities
- How to return plan to actual
- Executive summary

Join Together

Monitoring involves participation by the project team, contributors, resource managers, and stakeholders. Tapping these groups for their input will help you determine what is important to monitor and how frequently to monitor it. Although you (as the project manager) are responsible for project monitoring, each team member and contributor shares the load. Remember the ground rules you established in Start to Implement? They included how and when project information should be communicated to you, the project manager.

If you want these reports to contain targeted project monitoring data, share the chosen milestones with your team and contributors, as well as what will be monitored. This will help them to include relevant information in their status reports.

Reports will increase the likelihood of getting the right information in a timely way and ease the burden of preparing final reports.

The More You Know . . .

It may be that your organization relies on a specific tool to monitor a project. For example, *Earned Value Analysis* (EVA) is used in organizations to make specific calculations for time, cost, and performance to indicate current and anticipated project progress. For more information on EVA, see Additional Implementation Topic on pages 123–126. Other tools include Variance Analysis and Trend Analysis.

MODIFY THE PROJECT

Projects aren't perfect. Even though you invested a significant amount of time and effort in Definition and Planning, you still might be forced to make minor adjustments or wholesale changes as you implement the project.

As you and your project team monitor the project, issues and *concerns* will surface that need to be resolved. A concern can be a problem you need to solve, a decision that you must make, potential problems or opportunities you need to address, or additional actions you need to take. Modify the Project requires you to answer three questions about these concerns:

1. What is the data telling you about this concern?

   You first need to clarify exactly what the concern means. To do this, ask the appropriate project participants the following questions:

   - How was this concern surfaced?

   - When is the earliest point in the plan when it will become a concern?

   - What is meant by . . . (name the concern)?

   - What exactly is . . . ?

   - What evidence do we have about . . . ?

   - What different problems, decisions, or actions are part of this . . . ?

   - What else concerns you about . . . ?

Your answers to these questions will help you to separate and clarify concerns so that you are able to take action to resolve them. See Situation Appraisal on page 176 for more information on how to separate and clarify concerns.

2. What should you do about the concern?

You've captured and clarified concerns. Now you'll need to decide how to handle them. Does the concern require you to make a decision or solve a problem? If so, who will need to be involved and when? Or does the concern require that an action be taken? Who should take the action?

In some cases, you'll struggle to decide which concerns should be resolved immediately and which can be delayed until a later time. The Situation Appraisal method on page 176 offers a process for prioritizing your concerns by considering their current impact, future impact, and time frame.

Once you've clarified and prioritized your concerns, decide what actions to take to resolve them.

3. How will this impact the project plan?

4. Will you change the project objectives? Rearrange the project schedule? Launch a new project? Change the entire scope of the project? Request additional resources?

Depending on the action you take to resolve the concern, your project plan could be dramatically affected . . . or minimally tweaked. You need to decide how you'll edit your plan and how to best communicate the change to project participants and stakeholders.

Keep in mind that the cost of a change (in time and money) may not seem significant at first. However, a change that impacts even one project objective will most likely impact the WBS, the RAM, resource requirements, and the schedule of work packages. Before you know it, you're dealing with an enlarged scope and/or a woefully delayed project.

So, don't jump into a large change. Instead, consider more than one alternative for resolving your concern, and make sure you gain an upfront understanding of the cost and time ramifications of your change. When you decide to make a change to the project plan, however small, make sure you document it and the associated cost and time figures. This will allow you to evaluate the impact of all changes when you evaluate results at the end of the project. In addition, others can use the information to avoid the same problems in the future.

Modifying the project plan will also ensure that the project plan remains relevant and timely to the project team and contributors. If you don't modify the project, the effort you spent to create a guiding document that everyone follows and monitors will be wasted.

Example 4.6 shows the actual schedule versus the baseline schedule. Several modifications were made to the schedule to keep it on track. Work package 2.6 Office interior designed had to start earlier than planned because an interior designer had to be selected early enough to help identify equipment to keep (2.1) and equipment to order (2.4). The resignation of the facilities manager also delayed completion of the work package by eight days. This in turn lengthened the duration of work package 2.7 Equipment/office furnishings ordered from one day to eight days. And, although the start of 2.8 Equipment/office furnishings received was delayed by a day, it ended a day early thanks to the equipment being preordered. Other changes made, which impacted the budget by $8,000, were the purchase of fireproof filing cabinets in work package 2.7 Equipment and office furnishings ordered and new customized opportunity management software in work package 3.3 Computer services installed.

Join Together

Changing the project is a significant decision if it impacts the end result, the completion date, or the budget. Therefore, it's necessary that you involve customers and stakeholders in the decision.

Example 4.6   Actual Schedule

Project Statement

Move the Corporate Customer Services Department within three months at a cost not to exceed $170,000.

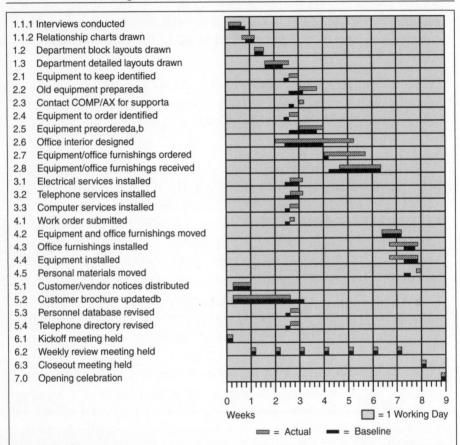

Work Packages	Gantt
1.1.1 Interviews conducted	
1.1.2 Relationship charts drawn	
1.2 Department block layouts drawn	
1.3 Department detailed layouts drawn	
2.1 Equipment to keep identified	
2.2 Old equipment prepareda	
2.3 Contact COMP/AX for supporta	
2.4 Equipment to order identified	
2.5 Equipment preordereda,b	
2.6 Office interior designed	
2.7 Equipment/office furnishings ordered	
2.8 Equipment/office furnishings received	
3.1 Electrical services installed	
3.2 Telephone services installed	
3.3 Computer services installed	
4.1 Work order submitted	
4.2 Equipment and office furnishings moved	
4.3 Office furnishings installed	
4.4 Equipment installed	
4.5 Personal materials moved	
5.1 Customer/vendor notices distributed	
5.2 Customer brochure updatedb	
5.3 Personnel database revised	
5.4 Telephone directory revised	
6.1 Kickoff meeting held	
6.2 Weekly review meeting held	
6.3 Closeout meeting held	
7.0 Opening celebration	

Weeks: 0 1 2 3 4 5 6 7 8 9

☐ = 1 Working Day

▨ = Actual   ■ = Baseline

ªPotential problem analysis revisions.
ᵇPotential opportunity analysis revisions.

CLOSEOUT AND EVALUATE

The project is finished, but is your work done? Not yet. Closing out a project involves several activities to review and evaluate the external and internal success of the project.

To determine how the project performed, consult your objectives first. After all, the objectives represent the goals you said that the project should meet. Then, compare them to the completed deliverables—the outputs of your project. Did the project deliverables satisfy the objectives? If they did, congratulations to you and the project team; you accomplished the most important part of the project. If you fell short, record why and what needs to be done about it.

TIP

Include project closeout activities in your work breakdown structure to ensure that they are completed.

Now, forget about the external success for a second. Focus on how well you, the project team, and project contributors worked together to manage the project. To conduct a review of the internal functioning of the project, examine the following areas:

- Project schedule (on time or delayed?)
- Accuracy of the resource estimates
- Impact of resource availability or shortages on the project
- Timeliness and accuracy of reporting by the team
- Timeliness and accuracy of feedback provided to the team
- Individual performance of team members and contributors
- Internal obstacles that impeded project work
- Resolution of conflicts

PITFALL

Check to make sure the contingent actions, capitalizing actions, and triggers you set in "Protect the Plan" and "Enhance the Plan" are disabled—keeping them around might run up cost or cause other problems.

- Acquisition of new capabilities or skills
- What went particularly well and should be repeated
- What went particularly badly and shouldn't be repeated

A closeout checklist and questions that you can use to evaluate your project are shown on page 121.

Sometimes, problems in the way the project team worked together can cause a failure to meet objectives. If this is the case, make sure the information is captured. It's also quite possible that you met the objectives but experienced internal problems and successes that should be captured as lessons learned. Record these as well.

It seems obvious, but communicating the end of a project involves more than a mere, "We're done, folks!" To shut down the project, you'll need to close out any financial reporting you've maintained and release your project resources to other projects and day-to-day work. In addition, you should contact project team members, contributors, and stakeholders to let them know the project is complete (see Example 4.7 on p. 122).

TIP

At the end of a long project, it may be difficult to report on lessons learned. To prevent this from happening and to maximize input over the life of the project, project managers can ask for one or two things that have gone well and one or two things that could have gone better. At the end of the project, the project manager compiles them as lessons learned.

Team members and contributors should also be given closure—an acknowledgment of their contribution and a formal ending of their commitment to the project. A closeout party, an article in the organization's employee newsletter or on the intranet, or a scrapbook represent concrete means of providing closure for project team members. But it's also critical that team members receive an individualized summary of their contributions to the project and feedback over the life span of the project. Submitting this report to them and their managers will formally end the performance evaluation.

Finally, you'll need to document the above closeout activities. Include the project's performance against objectives, actual expenses versus the budget, actual timing compared to the schedule, and

Checklist 4.2   Closeout and Evaluation Checklist

Closeout Checklist

√   Deliverables all completed

√   Owners, sponsors, vendors notified of close

√   Team members recognized

√   Project accounts closed

√   Contingent actions disabled

√   Results documented

Closeout Questions

1. Did the project satisfy the project statement?
2. How well were customers, sponsors, and end users satisfied with the project?
3. If any requirements were not met, explain why.
4. How well were project objectives satisfied?
5. How well did this project stay on schedule?
6. If any major deliverables were early or late, explain why.
7. How well did the team adjust to schedule changes?
8. How well did we estimate resources overall?
9. How did our actual use of resources compare to the plan?
10. How did changes in resource availability affect overall implementation?
11. How well did the team work together?
12. How were performance expectations set and maintained?
13. How well were performance expectations satisfied during the project?
14. What, if any, changes were made to the project definition after implementation started? Why?
15. What, if any, changes were made to the project plan after implementation started? Why?
16. How will you improve the next project you do?

Example 4.7   Closeout Report

Subject: Closeout Report   September 3

To: Corporate Customer Services Project Team

From: Tim Dwight

The Corporate Customer Services department has been installed in its new offices within three months, as planned. We exceeded the equipment budget of $70,000 by $8,000. This was due to the purchase of fireproof filing cabinets and opportunity management software. Both these items were added at the request of Peter Baldwin, the corporate customer services vice president, and were not on the initial equipment list. We also overran initial estimates on interior design labor costs by $4,216 because it took much longer to identify the equipment to keep and order (2.1, 2.4) and to design the office interior (2.6).

Had we not had a change in facilities management leadership, our original estimates would have been nearer the mark. The overall project cost came in at $177,209, which was $11,726 over the baseline and $7,209 over the $170,000 target set in the project statement.

Most of the work packages were completed either early or on time, with the notable exception of 2.6 Office interior designed, which ran eight days over schedule. This was due to the facilities manager resigning, a replacement having to be found, and then ramping up to complete the work.

To compensate, the duration of 2.7 Equipment/office furnishings ordered was increased to eight days from the original one day so that the material could be ordered as soon as decisions were made. This resulted in 2.8 Equipment/office furnishing received being completed on time. Thanks to some of the material being preordered, the work package was actually completed in 10 days instead of 11. The overall duration was 45 days, as originally baselined.

The project team and project contributors worked well together and were very flexible in rearranging their work schedules to accommodate the project schedule. All reporting was done in a timely fashion, and concerns were identified and reported to the person with primary responsibility as agreed on in the ground rules.

All vendor invoices have been paid by Finance and the project codes that were set up for this project are now in the process of being shut down.

Peter Baldwin has expressed his satisfaction with the way this project was completed. In particular, he was very impressed that service to customers was not disrupted during the move and that the COMP/AX computer was operational soon after it was set up in its new location. He intends to thank all project contributors at the opening ceremony scheduled for this Friday.

Documents pertaining to this project will be archived in the back office database by Sept. 23 and will be accessible to all project teams after that date.

lessons learned. This closeout document should also contain an executive summary, open issues, and any software files associated with the project. Archive these documents so that they are easily available to future project teams.

Join Together

Gather closeout data from everyone involved in your project—team members, stakeholders, customers, management, contributors, and resource managers—individually and in groups. You'll receive the most candid comments when you meet individually with people. Bringing the team and others together, however, allows you to see areas of consensus and disagreement. It can also spur the addition of forgotten or overlooked ideas.

The More You Know . . .

When you recognize project contributors and team members, it's probable you'll want to reward good performance. The more relevant and appealing a reward (or consequence) is to a person, the more likely he or she is to repeat the positive behavior. (For more information on people and performance, see "Influencing People" on page 133.) For example, if someone on your team is a hockey fan, an encouraging reward at the end of the project may be premium tickets to a local hockey game. However, avoid offering rewards that serve to demotivate project participants. For example, public recognition may seem like a positive consequence, but some individuals find being in the limelight embarrassing and therefore punishing.

ADDITIONAL IMPLEMENTATION TOPIC

Earned Value Analysis

Budget and schedule reports can tell you whether you've spent more money, or completed less work, or even finished in less time than planned. But they don't tell the whole story. What if you spent less money three months into the project than you planned? Is that good? Not unless you completed as much work as you expected. What if you

TIP

EVA relies on accurate and timely data to produce indicators. Make sure you have—or install—data-capture systems for relevant data, then check the key indicators regularly when monitoring.

completed more work in three months than planned? Is that good? Not if you spent more money than planned.

Examining budget and schedule reports may not be sufficient for you to accurately gauge project success. EVA will help you reconcile your spending and work completed by comparing them together . . . against the plan. Example 4.8 shows the breakdown of earned value elements and variances for the Corporate Customers Services project.

The elements of EVA include:

- *Planned value* (PV): How much did you budget for all the work packages that were supposed to be completed by now? In other words, how much should you have spent by this point?

- *Earned value* (EV): How much did you budget for all the work packages that we actually completed? The reason it is called *Earned Value: earned* because you've actually done the work; *value* because of how much you said it was worth when you budgeted for it.

- *Actual cost* (AC): How much did it actually cost to do the work you actually did?

Project variance represents how much your actual results are different from the plan. To calculate variance with EVA, use the following formulas:

$$EV - AC = \text{Cost variance}$$
$$EV - PV = \text{Scheduling variance}$$

Another EVA tool is a project performance index, which also gives you a better idea of how well your project performs. Calculate it with the following:

$$EV/AC = \text{Cost performance index (CPI):}$$
$$\text{1.0 or more means at or below budget}$$

$$EV/PV = \text{Schedule performance index (SPI):}$$
$$\text{1.0 or more means at or ahead of schedule}$$

Example 4.8   Earned Value Analysis

Work Breakdown Structure	PV ($)	EV ($)	AC ($)	SV ($)	CV ($)	BAC ($)	EAC ($)	Variance ($)
Move Corporate Customer Services	165,482.87	165,482.87	177,208.98	0.00	(11,726.12)	165,482.12	177,208.98	11,726.12
Office layouts	0.00	0.00	0.00	0.00	0.00	0.00	0.00	0.00
Office equipment	78,947.87	78,947.87	85,816.98	0.00	(6,869.12)	78,947.87	85,816.98	6,869.12
Office area	77,620.00	77,620.00	82,620.00	0.00	(5,000.00)	77,620.00	82,620.00	5,000.00
Office move	5,000.00	5,000.00	5,000.00	0.00	0.00	5,000.00	5,000.00	0.00
Organization manuals	2,915.00	2,915.00	2,772.00	0.00	143.00	2,915.00	2,772.00	143.00
Project managed	0.00	0.00	0.00	0.00	0.00	0.00	0.00	0.00
Opening celebration	1,000.00	1,000.00	1,000.00	0.00	0.00	1,000.00	1,000.00	0.00

Other calculations you can make using the previous figures:

- Dividing the CPI by the total project budget at completion (BAC) will estimate the eventual project cost.
- Dividing the SPI by the total project schedule at completion (SAC) will estimate the eventual completion time.

You can also forecast how much your project is likely to cost based on performance to date. This is known as estimate at completion (EAC). Three formulas can be used to calculate it. If variances on your project are seen as typical, use EAC = AC + BAC − EV ÷ CPI. If the variances are seen as atypical and no similar variances are expected, use EAC = AC + BAC − EV. If your previous estimates have to be revised substantially, then use EAC = AC + ETC (estimate to complete or the additional cost to complete the project based on performance to date).

Earned value analysis data can be represented in chart format (see Example 4.8) or as an S-curve (see chart that follows).

Total Allocated Budget

S-Curve Displaying Earned Value Analysis Data

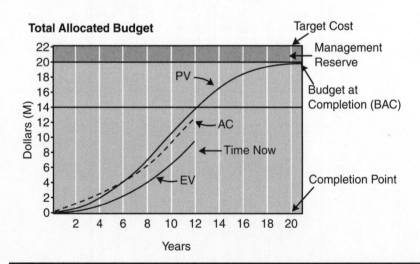

IMPLEMENTATION SUMMARY

This is it. This is when the work you and your team have done in Definition and Planning bears fruit—the results of the project become evident. But, as project manager, you aren't afforded the luxury to sit idly by and watch. Instead, you're tasked with monitoring and modifying the project and documenting successes and failures. After all, Publilius Syrus wrote, "It is a bad plan that admits no modification." And that was in the first century B.C. He was on to something. These activities are not only crucial to the successful completion of your current project but serve as valuable learning points for projects that you and your organization will undertake in the future.

chapter
5

managing people in projects

TIM DWIGHT CHOSE TERI Purcell to manage the interior decoration work package because he believed that she was the right resource for the job. The design activities appealed to her personally, and she had the right mix of experience and skills to manage the work successfully. But recruiting Teri's services wasn't easy. Tim spent several hours negotiating with Teri's manager for her time. Then he had to convince Teri that she wouldn't be "punished" for focusing on his project. Above all, Tim struggled with Teri's selection because he didn't have direct managerial control over her. If her manager reneged on his promises, or if Teri were pulled in other directions, Tim might not be able to influence and motivate her to accomplish his work. He also wondered whether to involve some of the key project contributors in the decision to use Teri and, if necessary, in managing her and her boss. He knew the contributors were bogged down already, and he didn't want this decision to morph into a major barrier.

How effectively you manage people is a crucial indicator of your project's success. Think of it this way: Your project has top management support; it is well defined, planned, and funded; you've done your homework around budget, time estimates, and assumptions; you've conducted thorough Potential Problem and Potential Opportunity Analyses; and you will manage the project using the latest and greatest tools that technology has to offer.

But no one wants to work on the project. And resource managers don't feel inclined to release their people to your project. And you favor unilateral decisions and tend to "disappear" when people need your input and guidance. If this is the case, your project will fail. It will fail even though you've mastered most of the fundamentals of project management. Why? Because, as stated at the outset of this book, project management, at its core, is about getting people to do "stuff" in a timely, organized, and effective manner. Getting people to do the "stuff" to define, plan, and implement the project is, quite simply, called *managing people in projects.*

Given its importance to the outcome of a project, you'd expect the literature, training curriculums, and skill sets directed to project managers to emphasize people management. There is an avalanche of material and courses on people management outside projects, and, as we've documented, there is more than a lifetime's worth on project management. But there is a surprising void when it comes to marrying the two. In fact, in our experience with hundreds of clients and thousands of projects, the majority of organizations approach managing people in projects as "something additional" when developing project managers and equipping them with the appropriate skills. As a result, many project managers and contributors are left to their own devices.

Not anymore. In this chapter, we tackle the three aspects of managing people in your projects: *Influencing, Involving, and Communicating:*

- *Influencing* will help you understand, create, and modify the conditions in a project environment that allow for successful human performance.

- *Involving* will guide you in determining the level of involvement you want others to have in your project decisions.

- *Communicating* will lay out the fundamental skill sets that a project manager must possess: from sound questioning skills to active listening.

In the "Join Together" section in Chapters 2 through 4, we began to explore ideas associated with managing people in projects. That was not an accident: Influencing, involving, and communicating should be woven into the fabric of any project management process. What's more, starting with a clear, visible, and rational approach to project management like the one described in this book will increase the likelihood that people will effectively complete work. So, throughout this chapter, we will return to the Define, Plan, and Implement approach to illustrate the power of managing people in projects.

INFLUENCING PEOPLE

What does influencing people mean in the context of your project? It means that, as project manager, you motivate and guide the behavior of everyone involved in the project—from those who report to you, to those who report to other managers, to those whom you answer to (such as stakeholders and customers).

However, influencing behavior is often easier said than done, which is why we recommend using a rational approach to increase the likelihood of getting the behavior—also known as performance—that you want from people involved in your project. We call this approach *The Performance System.*

TIP

Start with the belief that people on your team want to perform to the best of their abilities. People generally do not come to work intending to fail.

THE PERFORMANCE SYSTEM

The Performance System is a model for influencing human behavior. It can be used both to analyze the current performance of project participants and to construct a performance system for the people involved in your project. Tracing its roots back to the early years of behavioral science research by B. F. Skinner, we've validated it in numerous project and work environments. The five components of the performance system model are:

1. *Response:* The behavior (also known as performance) of the Performer.

2. *Performer:* The individual or group expected to behave/perform.

3. *Situation:* The immediate setting or environment in which a Performer works, such as the project environment.

4. *Consequences:* Events that follow the response and increase or decrease the probability the Response (behavior/performance) will occur again, given the same Situation.

5. *Feedback:* The information that Performers receive about progress toward their goals; it helps guide their Response (behavior/performance).

The components in the performance system model are not stand-alone parts. They are interacting and interdependent, as shown in Example 5.1. For example, in a particular Situation, a person or group takes a desired or undesired action (Response) that produces either wanted or unwanted results (Consequences) for the Performer, project, or organization. Information (Feedback) is provided to the Performer about the adequacy and appropriateness of the result.

TIP

When analyzing the performance system, gather information from the viewpoint of the Performer.

It's true that some project managers are naturals when it comes to applying this model; they provide pinpointed, timely feedback to contributors; motivate stellar performance with creative consequences; defuse conflicts before they occur by clearly setting roles and responsibilities; and generally excel at swaying stakeholders and customers. But even the most rational managers among us will occasionally rely on vague information and emotions to influence behavior. How many times have you witnessed yourself or others using labels like "unmotivated" or "uncooperative" or overheard a people problem being de-

Example 5.1   The Performance System Model

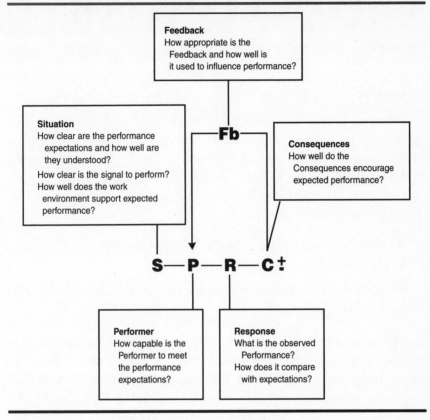

scribed as "a case of poor communication," "not seeing eye-to-eye," or "those fools over in Marketing dropping the ball?" How often have you been handed work and wondered, "What am I supposed to do with this?" And have you ever uttered the words, "So I guess my reward for doing this well is . . . more work."

These questions and statements all have their genesis in the Performance System. Looking more closely at each of the five components of the Performance System will help you pinpoint concrete, specific behavior that needs to be changed; identify its origins; and take effective action to replace it with more desirable behavior. In other words, together, they will help you *influence* the behavior of the people involved in your projects. We'll begin by taking an in-depth look at the Response, because changing behavior lies at the heart of this model.

Response

A Response is specific, observable behavior of a Performer. A Response can be influenced by Consequences, guided by Feedback, or exist as a result of the Situation. To put it simply, Reponses are the "stuff" that people do. To build or analyze a Performance System for your project, start with the behavior that you expect or want to see, then ask the following questions:

- What is the observed performance (Response)?
- How does it compare with expectations?
- What are the desired, the undesired, and the alternative Responses?

The desired Response is the behavior you want; the undesired Response, on the other hand, is behavior that you don't want. (An alternative Response is a behavior that you may want, but not in this particular situation.) For example, you'd like your team to arrive 15 minutes early to the project kickoff meeting so that you can actually begin at the start time. Some of them arrive 15 or more minutes early (the desired Response), while others actually show up as much as five minutes after the meeting start time (undesired Response). One person doesn't arrive at all (another undesired Response). Two individuals arrive exactly on time because they were busy collecting additional data for the project. This last behavior, arriving on time as a result of doing "extra" work, is an alternative Response. You want people to arrive on time for meetings, and you certainly want the extra data to drive the project plan creation. But for the kickoff meeting you really needed

TIP

When analyzing a human performance issue, begin with the action or behavior you have observed. This will allow you to determine whether performance needs to be modified and what needs to be changed in other components to resolve the issue.

everyone to arrive early to get the "how are yous" out of the way and start the meeting on time.

Responses should always be pinpointed: described in behavioral terms, free of generalizations or labels. The description of a behavior should be clear enough so that someone could replicate the behavior simply by reading it. This should be the case with the work-package descriptions that appear in your work breakdown structure (WBS). If you assign someone to a work package, it should be stated clearly and measurably. After all, it's tough for any resource to be successful when assigned a task that reads, "Produce a solid report" or when asked to "Be more of a team player."

Where possible, track behavior/responses over time to determine variations and assess the impact of changing behavior. Throughout the life of a project, from Define to Plan to Implement, you should be tuned in to the behavior of people associated with the project. This is the first step in being able to encourage more desired behavior and less undesired behavior (Example 5.2).

Performer

The Performer is usually an individual but may also be a team or larger organizational unit. After identifying the desired behavior or the behavior you want to alter, match it up with the appropriate Performer. For example, the desired Response is to reduce the amount of time required for weekly project status meetings. The Performers are the meeting facilitators.

Performance is more likely to be successful if the Performer has the capabilities to complete the specific task or project. The first question to ask to assess the Performer component of the Performance System is:

PITFALL

When faced with a performance issue, avoid jumping to a conclusion that the Performer is at fault. Do a quick analysis to see whether the other components of the Performance System are working as they should. Chances are, one or more of the other components are deficient.

- How capable is the Performer of meeting the performance expectations?

Example 5.2   The Performance System Example

The Performance System in Practice

Background: Project team members on a two-year project are expected to provide status updates on the first Wednesday of every month. Recently, reports from two of the eight team members have been tardy. Below is a performance-system analysis that the project manager conducted before coming up with a solution.

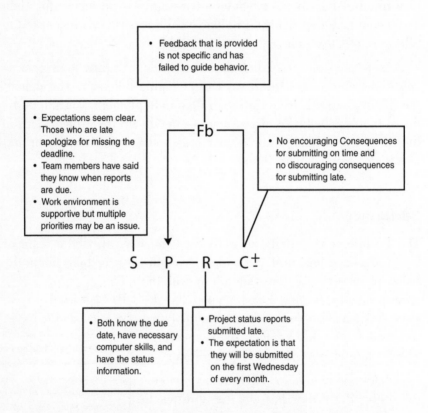

- Feedback that is provided is not specific and has failed to guide behavior.

- Expectations seem clear. Those who are late apologize for missing the deadline.
- Team members have said they know when reports are due.
- Work environment is supportive but multiple priorities may be an issue.

─ Fb ─

- No encouraging Consequences for submitting on time and no discouraging consequences for submitting late.

S — P — R — C$^{+}_{-}$

- Both know the due date, have necessary computer skills, and have the status information.

- Project status reports submitted late.
- The expectation is that they will be submitted on the first Wednesday of every month.

Solution: Modify the Situation by making sure "submitting reports on time" is attainable and that the priority is understood. Provide more immediate, encouraging Consequences and supportive Feedback on all aspects of the status reports. Emphasize value of the reports for sponsors.

If you find that your answer is too general, try asking these additional questions to obtain more specific information:

- Does the Performer have the necessary knowledge and skill to perform?
- Does the Performer know why the performance is expected?
- Is the Performer well suited to the job?

Assigning work to people who aren't qualified will delay and disrupt a project, so these questions should help guide your selections in the Assign Responsibility step of project management. But beware: Assessing the Performer component of the Performance System requires care. While the evaluation of knowledge, skill, and understanding may be completed objectively, avoid making assumptions about the nature of individuals and how well suited they are to the job. Assessing the physical, emotional, and intellectual limitations of a Performer is not only difficult but may be illegal.

Developing solutions to problems with the Performer also requires a careful touch. Consult with the Performer and his or her manager about the best ways to achieve the appropriate levels of knowledge, skill, and understanding to contribute to the project.

TIP

You'll see two question types for each performance system component. The first are open questions to guide the analysis and gather information. The second are specific, closed questions that focus the analysis. Both types help reveal performance system deficiencies.

You may choose to accommodate personal difficulties, particularly if they are temporary in nature, but keep in mind that you, as project manager, are responsible for delivering the project's results and for working within the project's constraints. In cases of a clear and continuing mismatch, ask the Performer's manager for a substitute or obtain a contract resource. Such a situation may raise problems, especially if the Performer outranks the project manager, is highly regarded, or is the only resource available.

Situation

No project's Performance System is complete without a careful examination of the Situation component, from the first steps of the project management process (Define and Plan) to the last (Implement). The Situation refers to the immediate environment or setting in which the Performer works: the project team to which he or she has been assigned or the particular function, department, or unit of which he or she is a member.

The Situation is made up of three key elements: performance expectations, signals to perform, and the work environment. Each element of the Situation impacts a person's or a group's behavior. If the Performer does not know or understand what is expected, he or she is

TIP

Set performance expectations when assigning responsibility and then secure agreement during work negotiations.

unlikely to perform as required. If the cues or signals to perform are difficult to detect or interpret, the Performer may be unable to recognize when a Response is required. If a person is called upon to perform two conflicting tasks, it may be impossible to do either satisfactorily. And if job procedures or limited resources make good performance difficult, the project will limp along.

To increase the probability that the Performer will act as expected, assess and consider adjusting each element of the Situation.

Performance Expectations

These are the specific results, measures, and standards desired of the Performer in completing the work. For example, "Action: Answer

TIP

If you're building a performance system for an upcoming project, you have an opportunity to create (rather than adjust) performance expectations, signals, and work environment.

the questions in this e-mail in 50 words or less by Monday, June 7. Include data in the responses to back up your opinions, and please respond using e-mail." These instructions act as performance expectations for the task.

Performance expectations should be familiar by now. They were addressed on page 62, as part of the creation of the WBS.

What's more, the initial work negotiation, recommended on page 61, details how performance expectations should be communicated to the project contributors.

Given their importance, there should be no confusion regarding performance expectations. In order for expectations to be clear, the Performer not only needs to know what is to be done but which aspects of the performance are most important to the organization. Consider the three pillars of the project management process: time, cost, and perfor-

mance. When setting and communicating expectations, include how each will be *measured* and which is the priority. Measures define the dimension or aspect of performance that is critical, while *standards* set the specific level of performance (stated in terms of the measure). For example, for a purchasing coordinator involved in processing equipment orders for your project, a quality measure could be "Number of accurate orders processed." The standard for this measure could be "100 percent." Or a timeliness measure could be "Number of days to process the orders." The standard here could be "Within two days."

To assess the quality of your project's performance expectations, ask the following question:

- How clear are the performance expectations, and how well are they understood by the Performers?

A more detailed analysis can be completed by asking:

- Have performance expectations, including measures, been established for the desired Responses?
- Have performance expectations been clarified with the Performer?
- Does the Performer agree that these expectations are attainable?

Signal to Perform

This is a cue or indicator to the Performer that action needs to be taken. For example, "When I send out the voice mail announcing the product launch, call the station manager immediately and start the radio campaign." The voice mail acts as the signal to start the radio campaign.

Signals should be overt and tangible if they are to be easily understood. The project schedule is one very strong signal for Performers to start the work. Others are the kickoff meeting, status reports, and Feedback. Clear, recognized signals should also be associated with the Modify Project step in project management: The project manager can use a change procedure to signal to project contributors that their work or focus should change.

Signals are most effective when they are built into the job or project (as milestones, for example) and do not require judgment on the part of the Performer (an automatic "pop-up" when work has moved beyond an assigned date).

Begin assessing the clarity of your signals by asking:

- How clear are our signals to perform?

A binary question can be used to understand the nature of each signal, its visibility, and its clarity:

- Can the Performer easily recognize the signal to perform?

TIP

Studies by human performance technologists like Thomas Gilbert (*Human Competence: Engineering Worthy Performance*, New York: McGraw-Hill, 1978), Geary Rummler and Alan Brache (*Improving Performance: How to Manage the White Space on the Organization Chart*, San Francisco: Jossey-Bass Inc., 1995), and others indicate that the majority of performance improvement opportunities are to be found in the performance environment: Situation, Consequences, and Feedback.

Work Environment

The Work Environment contains many pieces, from the process flow of a task to the priority of the work to the comfort of the physical surroundings. For example, "You will be provided with two contractors to test the user interface; you will have exclusive rights to their time, as well as to the computer room, for one week." In this case, the contractors represent the resources necessary to complete the job, and priority for their time is set: It's been given exclusively to you. You've also won the rights to the computer room as a resource.

The first question you should ask to assess your work environment is:

- How well does the work environment support expected performance?

You're likely to get many answers to this general question, so we suggest asking some additional, binary questions to pinpoint performance system deficiencies related to the work environment:

- Is the input the Performer receives appropriate, correct, and timely?
- Are job procedures and work flow effective?
- Have multiple or competing priorities been clarified? Has sufficient priority been assigned to the desired Response?
- Are adequate resources available: time, people, money, information, tools, or support equipment?
- Do the physical surroundings support effective performance?

The questions you ask about the Situation go to the heart of the Plan stage of the project management process. They address how work is planned, which work is more important, and what resources will be available to accomplish the work.

Consequences

Once you've identified the Performer, the Response, and the Situation in which the Performer works, it's time to evaluate the associated Consequences.

Consequences are events or conditions that follow a Performer's Response and increase or decrease the probability that the Response will occur again, given the same Situation.

There are two types of Consequences that impact behavior: encouraging—or positive—Consequences and discouraging—or negative—Consequences. The former reinforce behavior and increase the probability that a particular Response will occur again: When the project team completed the week's work by noon on Friday, it got the afternoon off; the Consequence acts as a reward. The team would be encouraged to work efficiently and finish by noon on Friday every week.

Discouraging, or negative, Consequences reduce the probability that a Response will occur again. If, for example, the team members stay late one Friday to complete the week's assignments—a desired behavior, to be sure—and the project manager comes by at 4:30 P.M. to assign weekend work, the office will probably be vacated by 4:00 P.M. the following week. The negative, or punishing, Consequences of the desired Response will keep the behavior from being repeated.

PITFALL

The Consequences a Performer receives may actually encourage Responses other than the one you want. The Consequences you put in place should be heavily weighted toward encouraging the desired Response.

Do not assume that because a particular Consequence is well intended, it will have a positive effect on performance. For instance, a Performer may accomplish one of his or her work packages well ahead of schedule. If the project manager then assigns this Performer additional work packages, perhaps those that are behind schedule, the individual may not welcome the new challenge. Instead, he or she may resent the additional workload and be sure to complete future assignments exactly when they are due and not a moment before!

The only way to tell if a Consequence is operating as it was intended is to observe subsequent behavior. If a Response is followed by Consequence X, and that Response occurs again, you can begin to assume that the Consequence is an encouraging one. If a Response is followed by Consequence Z, and that Response disappears or its frequency drops dramatically, you may start to conclude that the Consequence is a discouraging one, even if it wasn't intended as such.

Begin your assessment of the influence of Consequences within the Performance System by asking:

- How well do the Consequences encourage the expected Response?

Additional, binary questions can pinpoint potential deficiencies in Consequences:

- Are the Consequences immediate enough to encourage the desired performance?

- Are appropriate Consequences provided consistently?

- Are the Consequences significant to the Performer?

- On balance, do the Consequences encourage the desired performance?

- Do any of the positive Consequences to individual Performers carry negative consequences for the overall organization?

While it may not always be possible to ensure only positive Consequences for desired Responses/performance, you can usually influence performance by adjusting, adding, or aligning Consequences. The goal is to provide Consequences that are relevant and timely to an individual or a group of Performers. Because you don't always have supervisory-level responsibility for project contributors, think beyond traditional rewards, such as money and time off. Several books and articles suggest creative Consequences. One of the best is *1001 Ways to Reward Employees* by Bob Nelson (New York: Workman, 1994).

Consider the Balance of Consequences as you Assign Responsibility for work in the project plan (perceived encouraging Consequences for completing the work); as you Schedule Resources with the contributor's manager (ensure that the contributor will not be punished for working on your project); as you Start to Implement the plan (check Consequences for completing the work and following the ground rules); and throughout implementation, as you modify the plan and the Consequence system with it. Sometimes, you may only be able to remove negative Consequences for desired behavior—but this can be a big help in limiting the obstacles to success for your project contributors.

Feedback

Feedback is the performance-based information that Performers receive about progress toward a goal, which guides them in maintaining or modifying their Responses/behavior.

Feedback is one of the most critical components in the project Performance System, because it compares actual performance (exhibited in Implementation) with expectations (established in Define and Plan). Developing effective Feedback mechanisms should be one of the first steps in influencing performance, since improvement will only be sustained if the Performer is able to detect progress. Feedback mechanisms are established in the Ground Rules activity of project management and are a reflection of how the project manager goes about communicating progress to project contributors and sponsors.

There are four major sources of Feedback:

1. *The job itself:* Noise, gauges, meters, charts, peer and customer reactions; these are usually not in the domain of the project manager.

2. *The Performer:* The person checking work against a standard.

3. *The monitoring system:* The project manager creates or uses a system to monitor the project plan for cost, time, and performance.

4. *The receiving system:* This is the department or unit that receives and uses the Performer's output, or the project sponsor or customer.

Feedback is often given inconsistently or, worse yet, it's nonexistent or related to the wrong expectation. Sometimes project contributors don't receive feedback until the end of the project, when it's too late to guide their performance. To help you master the art of feedback, here are the characteristics of effective feedback:

- *Frequent and timely:* Generally, the more frequent the Feedback, the greater the possibility of keeping the Performer from drifting off target. Delays in Feedback on performance are costly because substandard work continues to be produced during that interval—especially troublesome when the project plan is a tight one. As time passes, the Feedback is less and less likely to eliminate the undesired Response. The Performer may have difficulty remembering specifically what went well or poorly or relating proposed solutions to the performance in question.

- *Relevant:* People will respond to whatever is measured and communicated to them. While Feedback should be provided against all performance expectations, not every performance expectation needs to have measures. It is better to determine which expectations are most relevant and significant to the task. When performance is in jeopardy because of outputs or behaviors, the leader should focus on more detailed measures and provide Feedback accordingly.

  However, it is important to measure *all facets of relevant performance.* Measuring only cost will be detrimental to other important dimensions of performance, such as quality, quantity, and timeliness. Feedback should be objective information from an unbiased source, assessed against an agreed-upon standard, and showing progress toward that goal. If the Feedback is delivered in a critical way, it may act as a negative Consequence, causing the Performer to react emotionally and defensively instead of replacing the undesired Response with a desirable one.

- *Specific and accurate:* Feedback must be specific if it is to impact behavior. The comment "Nice job," for example, does not tell the Performer about the details or trends of performance and what to do the next time to repeat success. Likewise, pinpointing evidence of inappropriate behaviors or actions is more likely to guide improvement than using terms like "unsatisfactory," or "inadequate."

- *Noise-free:* Useful feedback is often mixed with irrelevant details or buried in massive amounts of data. This "noise in the system" frequently masks useful

TIP

The *information* provided about performance is what differentiates Feedback from Consequences. The Performer will find the information valuable only if its accuracy can be trusted.

information. For example, a project manager receives numerous computer printouts each week, containing extensive data on the progress of various projects. While certain pieces of information on the printouts indicate the effectiveness of project activities and are extremely valuable, the effort required to retrieve them seems greater than the possible benefit. Hence, the project manager lets the printouts pile up unread.

> **PITFALL**
>
> When giving Feedback, pay particular attention to the tone of your voice and your choice of words. Both can have a significant impact on how a message is received and interpreted.

- *Confirmed by the Performer:* Feedback is valuable only if it results in the Performer maintaining or modifying his or her Responses. For this to take place, the Performer must agree with and accept the Feedback. When the source of Feedback is a gauge, chart, or information system, the Performer must be able to confirm the accuracy and completeness of the data. When the Feedback is given by another person, both people should discuss and confirm the information and its interpretation before actions are agreed to.

A good beginning question to assess the Feedback component of your Performance System is:

- How appropriate is the Feedback, and how well is it used to influence performance?

Here are more specific questions to help analyze Feedback:

- Does the Performer receive any information about performance?
- Is the Feedback used to encourage the desired performance/ Responses?
- Are relevant measures of performance being fed back?
- Does the Feedback include information about progress over time (e.g., over the course of a project)?
- Does the Performer receive timely Feedback?
- Does the Performer receive Feedback frequently enough to maintain or enhance performance?

- Does the Feedback include information about the value of the performance to the organization?
- Is the Feedback communicated in a positive, nonthreatening manner?
- Is the Feedback specific enough to influence performance?

One of the challenges of adjusting or creating a Feedback system to improve performance is to ensure that information is provided in a context relevant to the Performer. The project manager and Performers (project team, project sponsors, project contributors) should collaborate to design the most appropriate mechanism.

A Final Word about Influencing

Behavioral science is not a perfect, or even predictive, pursuit. Rather, it seeks to influence behavior by looking beyond the individual to the other, more significant components of performance. Although it's true that you can't change an organization's culture, you can increase the likelihood of seeing a specific behavior. By establishing a Performance System for your project, particularly around key work packages, you will improve your chances of success.

INVOLVING PEOPLE

Project managers are leaders in the truest sense of the word. They not only manage dollars and schedules but also influence and motivate people across all levels of the organization. Just as important, they shoulder the ultimate responsibility for the success of their projects and for the investment the organization has made in those projects. Under this kind of pressure, some project managers adopt an authoritarian leadership style, making decisions strictly on their own. Others bow to the consensus of their project team on every matter, stressing the importance of participation. Still others fall somewhere in the middle, deciding how much to involve others on a situation-by-situation basis.

Which type of leader behavior is best? The "project-manager-as-dictator" will fast grow irksome to project resources and other managers. And consensus among the ignorant is still ignorance. A situational approach to managing the involvement of others in project decisions is superior. But what criteria should a project manager use to determine the level of participation in a decision? What variables should impact the leader's behavior when it comes to selecting a solution?

Managing Involvement

The Managing Involvement process codifies the distinct types of leader behaviors "available" to a project manager. For example, you can choose to make a decision entirely on your own, with zero participation from others. Managing Involvement labels this "Resolve Alone" behavior. At the other extreme, you can choose to shift responsibility for resolution onto the group and participate as just another member. The Managing Involvement process refers to this as "Resolve as Group" leadership.

Being aware of the available leadership options is a good first step to managing the involvement of others, but it's fairly obvious. The real struggle arises when it's time to select a behavior for a specific situation. Accordingly, the Managing Involvement process also establishes seven factors that should impact the choice of behavior and arranges them into a decision tree. Walk through the Leadership Tree (Example 5.3) to find the appropriate leadership behavior for a number of situations.

The point of using the Managing Involvement process isn't to bog you down before you even start to examine the presenting situation. Rather, it's to give you a visible process that will increase the likelihood of getting the appropriate amount of involvement.

Leader Behaviors

There are five types of leader behaviors. Each behavior represents a different degree of participation for the project manager when it comes to making decisions, resolving situations, and gauging participation. The five leader behaviors are:

Example 5.3   The Managing Involvement Leadership Tree

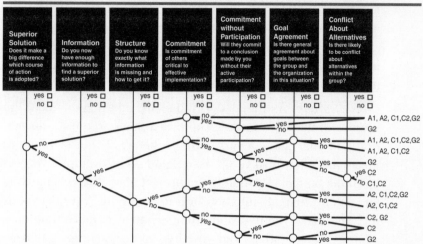

1. *Resolve alone:* As the leader, you resolve the issue alone, using the information currently available. Your behavior is time efficient, autocratic, and requires no participation. It's referred to as "A1" behavior. For example, you quickly select a resource to capture meeting minutes for all of your project team meetings. Obviously, a minimum level of analytic skill is required to resolve a situation alone.

2. *Question individuals:* As the leader, you obtain *information* from the appropriate person(s) individually and then resolve the issue. For example, you gather budget information from project contributors in order to determine how much additional funding will be required to complete the project. Questioning individuals is less time efficient, somewhat autocratic, and does not require the people involved to know anything about the issue or to participate in the analysis. It's referred to as "A2" behavior. Both analytic and questioning skills are required.

3. *Consult individuals:* As the leader, you explain the issue to the appropriate person(s) individually, request *information and analysis,* and then resolve the issue alone. For example, you present the budget crunch situation to each member of your

project team and ask for individual budget numbers and his or her input into how to best resolve the situation. Then, you make the decision on your own. Your behavior is less time efficient, consultative, and requires more participation from other individuals. It's referred to as "C1" behavior. Analytic, questioning, and listening skills are required.

4. *Consult group:* As the leader, you share information about the issue with the appropriate people as a group, request information and analysis, encourage an exchange of information and ideas, and then resolve the issue alone. For example, you explain the budget situation to the project team during a meeting and ask for insights into how best to resolve it. After the meeting, you make the decision. Your behavior is more time consuming, consultative, and requires more participation from other individuals. It's referred to as "C2" behavior. Analytic, questioning, listening, meeting-management, and conflict-management skills are required.

5. *Resolve as group:* As the leader, you share information about the issue with the appropriate people as a group, after having set ground rules for the meeting and criteria for an acceptable solution. You are part of the group and agree to accept and implement the group's conclusions. The group works together to resolve the issue. For example, you ask your project team, as a group, to resolve the budget crisis. They determine that the best solution is to go back to the project customer and ask for $100,000 in additional funds. You accept the recommendation. Your behavior is the most time consuming, consensus oriented, and requires the most participation from other individuals. It's referred to as "G2" behavior. Analytic, questioning, listening, meeting-management, conflict-management, building-consensus skills, as well as skills in setting group boundaries are required.

Categorizing the different types of leader behavior accomplishes several things for a project manager. First, it sheds light on the numerous styles you can choose to adopt in a situation. Second, it helps you analyze what behaviors you've used in the past and which may be appropriate for the future.

The Involvement Process

Determining which leader behavior to exhibit—and therefore how much participation you'll rely on—comes down to two major factors: the need for a *superior solution* and the strength of *commitment* required for the solution to succeed.

A superior solution is one where the course of action adopted will make a big difference to the outcome of a given situation. A superior solution is also consistent with organizational goals and strategy and is arrived at based on the best possible project data, information, and judgment. For example, a superior solution would be needed if a work package on the critical path of your project fell behind schedule. You would be faced with several options for bringing it back to date, each of which had its own pros and cons. In such a case, the best or superior solution would be essential.

On the other hand, if you needed someone to jot down meeting notes, it's quite likely that each of the meeting participants could handle the task with some degree of success. A superior solution to deciding "Who should record the meeting minutes?" is not required.

Once you've determined if a superior solution is necessary, move on to the commitment factor. In some situations, commitment is needed for the resolution to be successfully implemented. Consider the following example: Your project requires the selection of an Enterprise Resource Planning software system. Some key people in the organization will need to be committed to the system and vendor that you select, or the successful implementation of the software will be very unlikely. In this case, a superior solution is needed, and the commitment of the key people is also required.

But commitment is not always a must. Sometimes, people don't particularly need to be committed to a solution to implement it. Or they merely need to comply with a decision for it to be successful. For example, expense-account guidelines usually only require compliance (and not commitment) because people will follow the rules if they want to get reimbursed.

When commitment is required for successful implementation, the next step is to consider whether participation alone will generate that commitment. In some instances, people will commit without being involved because they perceive the leader as the expert or as the person who's supposed to resolve the situation. At other times, people won't commit unless they have actively participated in resolving the issue.

To assess how the need for a superior solution and commitment/participation play a role in selecting the appropriate leader behavior, follow a three-step Managing Involvement process.

Step 1: Define the Situation

The way in which you define the situation determines both who will be involved and how they will participate. For example, to "implement fire-prevention procedures" you may require the commitment of the group (C2 or G2 behavior), whereas to "find the cause of yesterday's fire" you may need to question individuals (A2 behavior). To develop a clear, concise definition of the situation, ask yourself "What specific concern needs to be resolved?" "What end result needs to be achieved?" or "What decision needs to be made?" Record the situation statement.

Step 2: Assess the Variables

Variables are characteristics that change from situation to situation. To be a successful project manager, you should consider seven key variables to determine the degree of participation needed. They are:

- Superior solution
- Information
- Structure
- Commitment

- Commitment without participation
- Goal agreement
- Conflict about alternatives

Assess the seven key variables using the Leadership Tree format by asking one closed question for each. The yes or no responses will direct your course through the tree "branches." Eventually, you'll arrive at the end of a branch, where a leader behavior or behaviors are recommended. Ask the following questions for each of the variables:

- *Superior solution:* Does it make a big difference which course of action is adopted?
- *Information:* Do you have adequate information to analyze this situation?
- *Structure:* Do you know exactly what information is missing, how to get it, and how to analyze it?
- *Commitment:* Is the commitment of others, either for judgment, action, or creativity, critical to effective implementation?
- *Commitment without participation:* Will others commit to a conclusion made by you without their active participation?
- *Goal agreement:* Is there general agreement about goals between the group and the organization in this situation?
- *Conflict about alternatives:* Is there likely to be conflict about alternatives within the group?

For example, if you're asked to purchase an important piece of production equipment, and you don't have a good understanding of the production process, you would answer "Yes, it does make a big difference which course of action I adopt," and "No, I don't have enough information to find the superior solution."

PITFALL

Do not fall into the trap of thinking that every situation requires a superior solution. Often, the second-best solution is good enough and has the added advantage of being quicker to implement.

Step 3: Select the Behavior

By stepping through the variables, you can determine which leader behaviors are likely to succeed in a given situation.

The Leadership Tree usually results in more than one suggested leader behavior. Any one of the recommended behaviors has the potential for success. The one you use will depend on the time available, the development needs of individuals and work teams, and other factors such as skills, geographic constraints, and the potential for things to go wrong or better than expected.

A Final Note on Involving People

The project manager who possesses a combination of sound influencing skills and a keen sense of when and how to involve others is well on his or her way to becoming a highly effective manager of people. But there's another piece of the equation, and that missing piece can make or break a project manager's ability to handle people and their issues. The third fundamental piece is communication.

COMMUNICATING WITH PEOPLE

The word communication has been tossed around enough, and there are plenty of soft skills available to project managers who need to improve their ability to "relate" to others. But for the purposes of managing people in projects, we will characterize communication skills as the ability to *ask questions and handle answers*.

To put it simply, project management consists mostly of gathering, organizing, analyzing, and confirming information. Your ability to manage will only be as good as the information you're using. Even the most robust project management software tool will be rendered almost useless without accurate, relevant information. This begs the question, "How can you improve the chances that the information you're using to manage the project is valid and reliable?" Your best allies, bar none, will be your ability to ask the "right" questions—

questions that probe for the type and scope of information you want—
and your skill in handling the answers.

Questioning

There are several basic types of questions you need to be aware of as
a project manager: open questions, closed questions, fact-finding
questions, feeling-finding questions, and questions to the void. Each
type is appropriate to particular situations; recognizing the situation
and crafting your questions to meet it will improve your ability to
communicate.

Open Questions

Open questions invite unrestricted answers. They're used to gather
or clarify new information and to stimulate involvement and thinking. The only limit that open questions impose is to confine responses to a defined topic, and therefore they may result in multiple
answers to the same question. Also known as *free answer, free
response,* or *unrestricted questions,* open questions usually start with
interrogative words such as "What," "Where," "When," "Who,"
"Why," or "How." For example, "What work packages are delayed?" or "Where in the schedule do you feel that the timing is too
aggressive?"

Closed Questions

Closed questions are used to elicit limited information. By design,
they often elicit a yes or no answer. Ask a closed question to confirm
or verify information, clarify something you're unsure about, limit the
choices offered, indicate a direction, or demonstrate understanding.
Also known as *binary, multiple choice,* or *restricted* questions, closed
questions usually start with interrogative words such as "Do,"
"Have," "Will," "Can," "Are," or "Is." For example, "Is John Smal-
ley the only person assigned to that work package?" or "Can we finish
the software installation before April 14?"

Sometimes people will answer a closed question as if you asked an open question. Be ready for a long answer, even though you want a short one.

Fact-Finding Questions

Use fact-finding questions to solicit specific, objective information rather than opinions, assumptions, or insights. To create a fact-finding question, choose your words so that they clearly ask for facts only. For example, "What specific evidence do you have that the marketing department is responsible for the late product launch?" or "Exactly how many dollars are we over budget?" Fact-finding questions can be very effective for a project manager who is overwhelmed with emotional people in a tough situation.

TIP

Facts are most likely to come from first-hand sources.

Feeling-Finding Questions

Unlike fact-finding questions, feeling-finding questions solicit subjective, sometimes emotional expressions of opinion or judgment. Again, choose your words carefully to ensure that the person you're questioning understands that you're looking for his or her opinion. For example, "In your opinion, what could have gone better about the first part of this project?" or "Why do you believe that Jane should be selected as the project manager?" Sometimes a project manager intentionally asks feeling-finding questions to allow project contributors to vent; after the emotion, he or she returns to fact-finding questions to focus the situation.

Questioning to the Void

This is a questioning strategy in which you ask a series of questions to extract as much *specific and complete* information as possible. The premise is that people often do not have all the information you need or will not volunteer it without rigorous questioning. After asking a series of such questions, you'll ultimately reach the "void," or the place where there is no further information you can gain from that source. At that point, you need to decide whether you have enough information to resolve your concern or whether to seek another source to fill in the gaps.

There are three types of questions used in this strategy: turnaround questions, "What else . . . ?" questions, and "Why . . . ?" questions. Ask all three types to elicit the information needed to make project concerns more specific and easier to resolve:

- *Turnaround questions* re-ask the question based on the answer. Use turnaround questions when you are searching for the most *specific* answer. When you stop making progress, you've reached the void. Example: "When can you complete the business plan?" ("Probably next week.") "When next week?" ("Sometime by the end of next week.") "When sometime by the end of next week?" ("By Thursday afternoon.") "When on Thursday afternoon?" ("3:30 P.M.") At this point, you've hit the void. You now know precisely at what time the business plan will be ready.

- *What else . . . ? questions* re-ask the question in the same form. Ask a "What else . . . ?" question when you are searching for the most complete information you can get about a concern or when you are seeking to break down a broad concern into more specific concerns. When you stop making progress you've reached the void. Example: "What concerns you about the pollution management project?" ("Fish are now dying.") "What else concerns you about the pollution management project?" ("The Department of Environmental Protection may fine us, adding to our already over-run budget.") "What else concerns you about the pollution management project?" ("We could receive bad press, which would reflect poorly on the project team.") "What else concerns you about the pollution management project?" ("Investors may withdraw their investments.") "What else concerns you about the pollution management project?" ("Nothing else.") At this point, there is no further information to be had about the pollution problem. You have completed separating your concern. You can now begin to determine which concerns to address, in

PITFALL

No matter what type of questions you are asking, be careful of your tone of voice when questioning: It can leave people with the impression that they're being interrogated or that they're involved in a strange verbal game.

which order. (See Situation Appraisal on page 176 for more on prioritizing concerns.)

■ *Why . . . ? questions* help you look beyond the problem or potential problem of the moment to ensure that you have identified its root cause. You may have only uncovered one symptom of a larger problem that, if not addressed, will continue creating the same or a similar problem. For example, suppose you're managing a new-product project, and one of the pieces of production equipment keeps breaking down, threatening your schedule. You identify the problem as, "Engine on Line #6 overheats." "Why does the Engine on Line #6 overheat?" ("The fan belt came loose.") "Why did the fan belt come loose?" ("Excessive machine vibration.") "Why does the machine vibrate excessively?" ("Don't know.") In this case, the company will change the fan belt but will also want to conduct a Problem Analysis, "Line #6 machine vibrates excessively" (see page 190 for more on Problem Analysis).

Although questioning skills may at first appear basic, a project manager who relies on assumptions isn't a project manager for long. The larger the project you manage, the more unfamiliar you will be with the pieces and parts. Solid and conscious questioning arms you with the tools to mine the necessary data and use that data to effectively manage the project.

Listening

Effective questioning is only one way of communicating with people. Active listening—the other component of communication—means understanding and acknowledging the full meaning of what the speaker is saying: both facts and feelings. It allows the listener and the speaker to relate, exchange information, and reach understanding. If you're not an active listener, your questioning strategy will fail because you will miss salient points in the conversation or ignore both verbal and nonverbal cues.

TIP

Thinking about something else when speaking with someone is often a dead giveaway that you're not giving the person full attention.

One of the critical aspects of active listening is that it's a conscious choice: You make the decision to listen or to do something else. Distractions caused either by noise in the environment, the speaker's use of language, or the speaker's tone of delivery can reduce your listening capability. There are four key elements to being an active listener:

1. *Hearing the message.* Active listening means focusing intently on the speaker's message. If you listen selectively, you can miss important information. Your values, interests, experience, emotional "deaf spots," and even the topic's importance influence how you filter information. Hold off interpreting the message until you've heard it completely.

2. *Interpreting the message:* Active listening involves understanding the speaker's verbal and nonverbal messages.

   - *Verbal cues:* Words can explain ideas, concepts, and experiences, but it's the listener who ultimately provides the meaning behind the words. Your biases, prejudices, assumptions, preconceived notions, pet peeves, and so on, can color your understanding of the message. Try to handle the information objectively.

   - *Nonverbal cues:* Gestures, facial expressions, eye movements, posture, proximity, body position, breathing, complexion, and energy level are signals to help you interpret a speaker's message. Inflection and tone of voice can convey more meaning than the words used. Be alert to inconsistencies between the speaker's nonverbal and verbal cues.

   - Verify your interpretation of verbal and nonverbal cues by paraphrasing what the speaker said, asking for clarification, questioning to the void, or providing feedback. There are usually a number of ways that a message can be interpreted. If you don't take the time to confirm your understanding, you run the risk of operating with faulty—sometimes even damaging—information.

3. *Evaluating the message:* Active listening doesn't mean automatically accepting what is being said. It means thinking critically about what you've heard and being sure you've got the whole picture before reaching a conclusion. Here are some "do's" and "don'ts" to help you evaluate messages:

Do . . .	Don't . . .
Get key information	Jump to conclusions
Gain commitment	Be compliant
Think analytically	Think mechanically
Listen actively	Hear passively
Consider facts and feelings	Consider only the facts
Be objective	Make a value judgment

4. *Responding to the message:* An active listener provides both verbal and nonverbal feedback when responding to a speaker. Good listeners let the speaker know that the message has been heard, understood, evaluated correctly, and that they are prepared to follow up. When responding to a message, avoid being defensive, using the blank-stare approach, or sending a mixed message (e.g., inconsistency between verbal and nonverbal cues).

Handling Answers

Skillful handling of the answers to your questions is key to gathering and confirming useful information for your project. Handling answers means receiving and assessing information given to you by others. There are five components to handling answers: listening, acknowledging, confirming, recording, and providing feedback:

1. *Listening:* Use gestures and facial expressions such as making eye contact, leaning forward, and nodding your head to show

the speaker that you're interested in what he or she has to say. This creates a nonjudgmental atmosphere that encourages the speaker to keep speaking. In addition, make sure you give the speaker time to talk.

2. *Acknowledging:* Use nonjudgmental words and a neutral tone of voice to fill in the gaps when the speaker pauses. This shows that you are paying attention and encourages the speaker to continue speaking. To acknowledge, use words or phrases such as "Ah-hah," "Uh-huh," "Yeah," "I see," "I got it," "I understand," and "That's right."

3. *Confirming:* Paraphrase what the speaker said, in your own words, to confirm the answers to your questions. This shows the speaker that you understand what he or she has said and enables you to check for mutual understanding of the facts. Phrases that will help you practice this technique are: "What I hear you saying is . . ." and "If I understand you correctly, you think that . . ."

4. *Recording:* Document the speaker's message by writing the information on a notepad or easel or recording it in the appropriate place. This has two benefits: You remember the important details of the conversation, and you give the speaker the impression that his or her information is valuable.

5. *Providing feedback:* Give the speaker feedback about the usefulness of his or her message. This helps the speaker understand what changes, if any, need to be made to the message. Phrases to use when you provide feedback are: "What you gave me was useful because it . . ." and "The way you organized the information was useful because . . . "

Sometimes an answer is confusing or isn't responsive to the question asked. This could be because the person you asked interpreted the question incorrectly or because your intent was not clear. For example, you ask, "Have you seen Robert today?" The person, guessing at what you want to know, answers, "He hasn't submitted his report yet." To get the information you need, clarify the intent of your question, then ask it again. Respond, "I have to speak to Robert about the problem with Line #6. Have you seen him today?"

At other times, an answer may raise doubts about how the person you asked got his or her facts. For example, you ask, "When did the schedule delay start?" The person answers, "They said it started last Tuesday." To be confident that this information is factual and to verify the credibility of the information, you should ask, "Who said that?" and/or "How do they know that?"

Incomplete answers may also cause problems. For example, you ask, "What are your objectives in choosing the computer?" and the person answers, "Processing speed." If you suspect there could be other objectives, use questioning to the void techniques to ask, "What other objectives do you have?"

Finally, the answer you receive may be too general. For example, you ask, "Why haven't you completed the report?" The information source answers, "I haven't had the time." This answer does not satisfy you, so you ask a turnaround question—"Why haven't you had the time?"—to get a more specific and useful answer.

A Final Word on Questioning

If relentless, focused questioning and active, serious listening were easy, everyone would engage in them. Thorough communication requires discipline: as much discipline as the "harder" skills of managing projects, such as learning software or leveling resources or building a WBS. Failing to follow through with people, however, can leave information uncovered and assumptions untested—dangerous potholes for the project.

MEETINGS AND COMMUNICATION

Meetings, meetings, meetings! For years, people involved in projects have ranked "time spent in meetings" as one of their top workplace complaints. Some of the most common shortcomings of typical meetings are:

- There is no clearly stated purpose for the meeting.

- Participants are ill-prepared.

- The right people are not present, or the people who are present have no real involvement.

- The meeting does not focus on one issue at a time.

- Results could have been achieved as well or better without a meeting.

- The meeting runs too long.

- The meeting dissolves rather than ends.

- Participants are unclear on the next steps following the meeting.

These shortcomings seem to exist no matter what the meeting venue: a conference call, a teleconference, even a virtual meeting. Use the approach outlined next to guide you in managing your project meetings, no matter what form they take.

Before the Meeting

Prior to the meeting, ask yourself and others four basic questions:

1. *What concerns do you have about conducting the meeting?* Answers to this question will help you plan and prepare for the meeting by developing an agenda, identifying who should attend the meeting, selecting the chairperson and facilitator, announcing the meeting, and resolving other issues that could threaten the success of the meeting.

2. *What concerns need to be addressed during the meeting?* Answers to this question will reveal the issues you want to resolve or appraise during the meeting. If necessary, set priority on these issues to determine which ones will be evaluated during the meeting. Record the concerns so that you can track their resolution. Some meetings, for example, may be held around a particular work package in the project plan or around a particular concern that threatens the entire project.

3. *Given your concerns, what do you hope to accomplish in the meeting?* Answers to this question should become your primary meeting objective—the specific, main goal you want to accomplish in a meeting—and your secondary meeting objectives. They will focus the meeting and help you determine how to best conduct it.

4. *Given what you hope to accomplish, who should be in the meeting?* Involvement is critical to securing commitment to your project. However, there are more ways to involve people than asking them to be present at a meeting. You can copy them on the meeting minutes, ask them to join in one specific portion of the meeting, debrief them personally afterwards, and so on.

The answers to these questions can serve as the meeting agenda. This will help prepare people for the meeting and, once it has begun, keep it on track. As onerous as people may perceive face-to-face meetings to be, there are still legitimate reasons for bringing people together. Here are some questions that will help you decide if a face-to-face meeting is necessary:

- Is a meeting the best way of reaching the primary meeting objective?
- What is the value of accomplishing the primary meeting objective?
- How else could the primary meeting objective be achieved (conference call, Web meeting, videoconference)?
- What would be the consequences of not holding a meeting?
- Is the meeting worth the cost?
- What could people be doing instead of meeting?

PITFALL

The cost of a face-to-face meeting includes attendees time, travel, and lost opportunities, in addition to the cost of planning, conducting, and following up on the meeting.

Preparing people for the meeting increases the likelihood that they will come with the necessary data to address the meeting objectives, thereby making the meeting more productive. Consider using the Consequences component of the Performance System to influence people to prepare for the meeting and to arrive on time.

During the Meeting

Some successful project managers start every meeting with a Situation Appraisal (for more on Situation Appraisal, see page 176) to ensure that all participant concerns are included, that the meeting addresses the most important concerns, and that the group agrees on the analysis needed. Concerns not addressed during the meeting can be carried forward to the next one or assigned for individual resolution. A quick Situation Appraisal is particularly useful at the beginning of a staff, departmental, or project meeting designed to cover a number of topics—as long as you track resolution on all issues and actions surfaced during the meeting.

Even if you don't use Situation Appraisal, separate the content of the meeting from the process of running it. In other words, don't let yourself become so bogged down in the content of a particular issue that you lose track of the meeting's objectives. Keep control of the agenda and help focus the group on what's important.

Parts of the Situation Appraisal process can be very useful during a project meeting. For example:

TIP

During the meeting, keep the results visible—it keeps people on track and helps capture issues and actions.

- Separate and clarify concerns raised during any meeting by using the questions "What do you mean by . . . ?" and "What else concerns you about . . . ?"

- Set priorities on concerns or actions using three dimensions: *current impact, future impact,* and *time frame* (for a description of each, see pages 178–180).

- Assign primary responsibility for actions to make sure they are completed.

TIP

Start an issue-registry list for your project. It contains the open issues and resolution plans for things that don't fit into your project plan.

And, if you complete the agenda early, end the meeting. This provides an encouraging Consequence for desired behavior.

After the Meeting

The most important thing you can do after a meeting is make sure that the results are communicated and that progress on actions is monitored. Ask the following questions, similar to those asked in Project Monitoring, to help track progress on actions:

- Have agreed-upon actions been added into the project plan?
- Are actions being accomplished by their target date?
- Are the results on target?
- Has the primary meeting objective been met? If not, what else can we do?

It may also be useful to conduct a postmeeting Situation Appraisal with attendees or members of the project team to identify what still concerns the group about a given situation. This will allow team members to contribute issues that have come to mind after the meeting or that were not given time during the meeting. It also helps ensure that follow-on actions are documented and assigned responsibility.

Involving People in Meetings: The Challenges

People who join your project meetings may present one or more of the following obstacles to the efficient, objective resolution of issues:

PITFALL

General descriptions such as "budget woes" and "communication difficulties" tend to lump together a wide array of concerns, effectively hindering the group's ability to resolve the concerns. Breaking down these descriptions into specific concerns is the first step to successful resolution.

- They are unable to communicate openly due to bias, hidden agendas, or competing commitments.

- They are unable to work around feelings and emotions that might influence their ability to manage or get along with others.

- They have a tendency to jump to conclusions about other people, the cause of a problem, or the best alternative for a decision.

- They want to assume responsibility for issues that lie beyond their skills and/or training.

- They describe concerns in broad terms or with general labels rather than with precise, specific language.

- They present rumor and opinion as fact.

- They are unfamiliar or uncomfortable with either the content under discussion or the process being used.

Sometimes, taking a step-by-step, clear approach to project and meeting management will force people to set aside their biases, unfounded conclusions, and emotions. But if you find that your meetings are constantly being derailed by such people, here are several methods you can use to overcome them:

- If people begin to discuss content that's related to another project or concern, let them know that what they are saying is valuable but not relevant to the current issue. Recording this information and promising to revisit it at the appropriate time will relieve the group's need to discuss it, while allowing you to stay focused on the issue at hand.

- Test information that's offered as fact. Questions such as, "How do you know that?" or "What is the source of this information?" or "What evidence do you have?" will test the validity of the information. These questions will also help reveal assumptions.

- Use proper questioning and listening skills to gather the correct, specific, and relevant information from others. Sometimes, using *proper* questioning means phrasing your questions so that everyone, regardless of their experience, understands what you're asking.

Meeting obstacles can also result in conflict. Even the best project management meetings and discussions may surface disagreements, which isn't necessarily bad. In fact, if managed effectively, conflict can bring important issues to light and facilitate the search for constructive solutions. Focusing the debate on facts associated with a specific issue—rather than on the emotions involved—will help you funnel the emotion into constructive discussion. Being clear about expectations and the commitment you require will also help avoid conflict.

TIP

Turn emotional expressions
into actions by summarizing
feelings and asking for specific actions to address the
issues.

If emotions are present but not brought to the surface, people can become resentful, and good working relationships can be destroyed. Allow people sufficient time to vent their feelings and explain their concerns. Giving them too much or too little time can be equally frustrating. Here are some methods for getting emotional obstacles out into the open:

- Let people vent their emotions. You relieve inner turmoil when you bring feelings into the open. This can be done by:

  —Using unstructured statements like "Something seems to be bothering you . . ."

  —Reflecting others' feelings by repeating their own statements back to them. For example, "You believe that . . ." or "You feel that . . . " This technique helps people to express their feelings more fully.

  —Not interrupting pauses, which can allow for expression of emotions.

  —Not answering emotionally loaded questions. These questions are not usually asked to gather information but are part of an emotional expression. Respond by reflecting on the feelings implied in the question or by asking a question in return.

  —Identifying the source of the emotions. Emotions can come from different places. Some arise from the discussion at hand. Others come from outside issues. Knowing the origin is the secret. If the dispute is outside the discussion's scope, it may be so identified and set aside for resolution later on. But if the issue relates directly to the immediate discussion, then the feelings must be resolved.

A Final Word on Meetings

Meetings don't have to be a brutal survival exercise. Proper preparation, execution, and follow up can actually turn your project meetings into a productive use of everyone's time. And this can help set your projects apart from others in the organization.

SUMMARY

Managing the people involved in your project requires specific knowledge, skills, and practice. It's not a task to be handled on an as-needed basis.

First, you need to understand your people: what motivates them and how they will react. Second, you need to understand and build, within the context of your project, a Performance System that will help people succeed. Third, you also need to determine when you will involve others, in what situations, and when you will go solo. Your decision to do this will be influenced by the situation, your need for a superior solution and/or the commitment of other players, and your time constraints. Fourth, whether you are gathering information, gaining consensus, or making further progress on your project, skills like questioning and listening will play a vital role in its success.

chapter
6

project decision making and problem solving

TIM DWIGHT'S PROJECT WAS making headway when things started to unravel around major deliverable 4.0: Office Move. Purchasing began to complain that they were experiencing "delivery problems" with the equipment ordered. Facilities Management called to say they were experiencing "personnel shortage problems" due to an employee having injured his back and the resignation of the facilities manager; now they are asking for the duration of several work packages to be increased. Most of these work packages are on the critical path. A majority of employees in the Customer Services department have been asked to support a major sales effort and think they may have problems packing their personal possessions by the specified deadline. The vice president of CORPORATE CUSTOMER SERVICES and the various department managers have sent Tim some conflicting messages about how quickly they want to move, despite having previously concurred on the project's time frame. Tim is beginning to get overwhelmed.

Sound familiar? Tim needs to appraise the situation before launching needlessly into action that will consume resources but might not resolve the various difficulties he's facing. First, he needs to better understand whether the concerns can be resolved by taking some immediate action or whether they need to be analyzed further.

The word "problem" surfaced several times in the opening paragraph and is being used to express very different concerns: a situation that requires action, something that has gone wrong and the reason is not known, a choice that has to be made. Each of these concerns requires a different approach. *Situation Appraisal* is a commonsense process for clarifying concerns, setting priority on those concerns, and making them manageable. *Decision Analysis* is an approach to making the best choice after considering the risks inherent in that choice. *Problem Analysis* is an approach to finding the true cause of a problem so the problem can be fixed permanently.

SITUATION APPRAISAL

Situation Appraisal is a step-by-step process that enables you to systematically identify, sort, and prioritize concerns. It is especially effective in a project management environment where you encounter many issues that compete for your attention.

Where to Use It

Situation Appraisal will be useful throughout Definition, Planning, and Implementation of your project. But here are a few especially valuable areas where you can apply Situation Appraisal:

- Producing the list of reasons for completing the project prior to writing the project statement.

- Identifying and clarifying the things that need to be completed or addressed during the project (prior to Definition).

- Listing concerns around how an objective will be met prior to developing the work breakdown structure or designing a work package.

- Clarifying concerns arising from project monitoring and other sources to better understand how your project plan should be modified.

- Creating and maintaining an "open" Situation Appraisal on issues that arise and are resolved during the life of the project. This will help you keep track of issues, resolutions, decisions, and changes and help you prepare status reports and a closeout report at the end of the project.

TIP

Most likely, your Situation Appraisal will require the input of more than one or two individuals. Involve the appropriate project team members, contributors, stakeholders, and experts to ensure that you capture all relevant concerns.

Steps in the Process

The first step in a Situation Appraisal is to establish a theme and time frame. The *theme* is a brief phrase that describes the target of your Situation Appraisal, and it can be general or specific. For example, if you're defining a safety-improvement project, your theme might be "All concerns we have about safety." Later on in the project, you might conduct another Situation Appraisal that's more focused, such as "The delay in the oil clean-up work package."

TIP

Situation Appraisal is one of the best tools to use at ad hoc or agenda-less project team meetings and for confronting concerns (whenever they may arise) with the project's progress.

Adding a time frame focuses the appraisal on a block of time because, as you are aware, information and priorities are constantly changing and need to be updated frequently. Restrict your Situation Appraisal to a time frame such as "this year" or "within the last quarter" or "this week" if it's appropriate.

After recording the theme and time frame, list all of your *concerns*. A concern can be a decision to be made, a problem that needs to be solved or prevented, an action that requires completion, or an opportunity that needs to be seized. Record everything that's revealed during this step, even if you're not sure it qualifies as a concern. However, avoid extended discussion or thinking about any one concern—this may indicate you've moved into analyzing the concerns. You'll create a plan for analysis later in the Situation Appraisal.

Now that you have a list of concerns, you'll need to obtain a better understanding of what they mean. To do this, rewrite the concern as one or more statements in which the meaning and the action required are clear. If you're not sure whether a concern should be separated or clarified, follow these guidelines:

- Separate a concern if it contains more than one issue or action. For example, the concern "Work package 3.1 is delayed and the output is poor quality" should be separated into two concerns—"Work package 3.1 is delayed" and "The output for 3.1 is poor quality."

PITFALL

As you separate and clarify your concerns, make sure the new and revised statements are factual. If you're not sure about the validity of a concern, ask, "What evidence do we have that this is an actual concern?" Trying to analyze concerns that aren't based on facts will waste your time.

- Clarify a concern if one of the words is vague or too general or if, as written, it doesn't tell you what action or process will resolve it. For example, look again at "The output for 3.1 is poor quality." This needs to be rewritten because it's unclear which output is of poor quality, and it's also unclear what "poor quality" means. After clarifying this concern, it might become "Research report did not include the requested executive summary." Now, the output is clear (research report) and "poor" is understood (missing an executive summary).

Example 6.1 is an example of listing, then separating and clarifying, concerns. The software installation project team uses Situation Appraisal to resolve concerns regarding why the project is behind schedule.

It's possible that after separating and clarifying your concerns you'll know which ones need your immediate attention and which can wait. But don't count on it. If you need an effective, rational way to set priority, consider these three measures:

- *Current impact:* What is the severity of the concern at the present time in terms of cost, quality, human resources, safety, or any other related criteria?

Example 6.1 Situation Appraisal—Clarification and Priority

Theme

The software installation project is behind schedule.

Concern	Clarified Concerns	Current Impact	R	Future Impact	R	Time Frame	R	Priority Rating
Some work packages are delayed.	Work package 4.1.4 "Upgrade skills of the IT department" has fallen behind.	Behind 4 days and counting. So far, we've spent $16,346 on contractors to cover for them.	H	We will spend $4,000 a day until they possess the skills. Project is to be about another 12 days delayed.	H	If we don't have the skills by April 14, the resources will have all been spent on contractor cost.	H	H
	Work package 14.2.5 "Receive new hardware" was delayed because it was damaged and we were forced to send it back.	Behind 6 days; cost us administrative time in evaluating it and sending it back.	M	No future impact on the outcome of the project's schedule or budget.	L	Potential to make the same mistake on the next project.	L	M
	Work package 8.4 "Hire database administrator" (DBA) is delayed.	Delayed by 14 days and counting.	L	Without a DBA the entire plan will begin to be delayed.	H	If we don't have a DBA by the end of June, we won't be able to complete the project.	M	L
Jim Flanders was reassigned.	Jim Flanders, a member of the project team, was reassigned to another project. We need a replacement.	He is responsible for 12 work packages. They have fallen behind by one day each. One of them is on the critical path.	M	We will not be able to install the software for our remote users without Jim's skills.	H	Every day it gets closer to impossible for someone to step in and assume Jim's responsibilities and still meet the project deadline.	H	H

- *Future impact:* What is the potential change in severity of a concern over time . . . Will the concern stabilize, get better, get worse, or disappear altogether? This is measured in terms of the anticipated change in cost, quality, human resources, safety, or any other related criteria.

- *Time frame:* What is the amount of time left before a concern becomes too difficult, expensive, impossible, or pointless to resolve?

Record factual information on the current impact, future impact, and time frame of each concern and then make your judgments as to which concerns are high, medium, and low priority for each area. Then, taking these ratings into account, assign an overall priority to each concern. Example 6.1 also demonstrates priority setting.

PITFALL

Not everything is a high priority. Although it may seem like every concern is screaming for your immediate attention, some are more important than others. Trying to handle them all at once may lead to failure.

The next step in Situation Appraisal pertains to the actions you'll take to resolve the concerns. There are several choices:

- If the concern indicates a need to make a decision, write a decision statement and conduct a Decision Analysis (see pages 181–190 for more about Decision Analysis).

PITFALL

Data will only help you set priority if it's specific. For example, instead of recording "losing money" as Current Impact, write "losing $75,000 a day."

- If the concern indicates that a problem needs to be solved, write a problem statement and conduct a Problem Analysis (see pages 190–195 for more about Problem Analysis).

- If the concern refers to a future problem, conduct a Potential Problem Analysis (see page 83 for more about Potential Problem Analysis).

- If the concern refers to a future opportunity, conduct a Potential Opportunity Analysis (see page 90 for more about Potential Opportunity Analysis).

- If the concern is an action, schedule it to be completed as a part of the project plan.

Sometimes, it's helpful to construct a "Resolution" column where you record how you plan to resolve the concern and why. In either case, the final step involves assigning the actions to project contributors or team members, with their agreement, and making sure you set expectations for the outcome in terms of time, cost, and performance. Example 6.2 on page 182 illustrates how to plan the resolution of concerns for the software installation project.

DECISION ANALYSIS

Decision Analysis is a step-by-step process that helps you make a choice. It's especially effective if you face a very complex or important decision or if you need to demonstrate the thinking that goes into your decision making.

Where to Use It

Use Decision Analysis to handle the many choices that arise during Definition, Planning, and Implementation. Here are just a few areas where you can use Decision Analysis in a project:

- Selecting a project manager
- Designing work packages
- Selecting capital equipment
- Determining the facility you'll use to complete part of the project
- Selecting vendors
- Choosing people for responsibility assignments
- Demonstrating the benefits and risks of any decision you need to present to stakeholders
- Choosing the most effective method and times for monitoring the project
- Selecting the best way to bring a project back on track
- Selecting the best way to acknowledge project contributors

Example 6.2   Situation Appraisal—Action Plan

Clarified Concerns	Process Needed	Resolution	Actions	Who	By When
Work package 4.1.4 "Upgrade skills of the IT department" has fallen behind.	Decision Analysis (DA)	Conduct a DA to select the best way to train the staff quickly.	Frame the objectives. Research the alternatives. Present recommendations.	John Smalley	March 30
Work package 14.2.5 "Receive new hardware" was delayed because it was damaged and we were forced to send it back.	Problem Analysis (PA)	Conduct PA on the cause of the damage.	Describe the problem. Find the cause. Implement the solution.	Sergi Zumonv	April 15
Work package 8.4 "Hire database administrator" (DBA) is delayed.	Situation Appraisal (SA)	We've already conducted an SA, but we haven't had luck finding qualified candidates.	Reopen the search.	Shirley Manderville	March 28
		We have concerns about getting this individual trained quickly.	Separate and clarify the concerns.		April 5
Jim Flanders, a member of the project team, was reassigned to another project. We need a replacement.	Decision Analysis (DA)	Conduct a DA to select a replacement for Jim.	Frame the objectives. Research candidates. Make an offer to selected candidate. Find a temporary replacement.	John Smalley	March 28
	Potential Problem Analysis (PPA)	Conduct a PPA to plan for the possibility of another person leaving the project or the company.	Find likely causes and take preventive action.	Shirley Manderville	March 25

Steps in the Process

The first step in Decision Analysis is to write a decision statement. Ask yourself (and others involved), "What are we trying to decide?" Phrase your answer into a decision statement starting with a choice word like "select," "pick," or "choose." For example, your project may involve conducting the company's annual sales conference and you need to decide which hotel will host the sales conference. Your decision statement might be, "Select a hotel to host our annual sales conference." Or maybe you have to select a resource to lead a particular work package, in which case your decision statement might be, "Select a resource to lead work package 12.1 Technical Manuals Produced."

TIP

Use Decision Analysis to determine which projects to work on. Your objectives should include strategic considerations, the anticipated results of "ideal" projects, as well as resource and other restrictions you face.

Once you've written the decision statement, list the *objectives* that describe the ideal outcome for your decision. Like project objectives, your decision objectives will contain results you want and restrictions you must adhere to.

For "select a hotel to host our annual sales conference," your list of sales objectives might include the following:

TIP

Objectives will have either a quantifiable measure or measures that are clearly understood. In either case, the measures should be documented.

- Minimizes cost per participant.

- Offers the most on-site dining options.

- Has a strong reputation for service (as measured by annual hospitality industry customer satisfaction survey).

- Maximizes seating in the main conference room.

- Has at least 200 rooms available next February 14 to 18.

There are a few things to keep in mind when writing decision objectives:

- A feature is a prominent aspect or characteristic of something. Decision objectives are not features . . . they are statements of benefit. For example, if you're choosing which car to buy, a feature might be "leather bucket seats." However, your true objective is "comfortable seats." Leather bucket seats are just one way to meet that objective.

- Each decision objective should be measurable, just like your project objectives. After you write an objective, add the phrase "as measured by . . ." to the end of it. This will help you think of how the objective should be measured.

- Decision objectives can draw on the project objectives, but they should never contradict them. Your project objectives represent overall goals for the project—writing decision objectives that contradict them will make it more difficult to reach your goals.

Now that you've written the objectives, separate them into two groups—*Musts* and *Wants*. Must objectives represent those that are absolutely mandatory, have a set limit, and are realistic. Want objectives, on the other hand, are those that aren't Musts. If you need additional details about how important each Want is to the outcome of the decision, rate them on a scale of 10 to 0, with 10 indicating the most important objectives. This is called the *weight*. Here's how you might rate the hotel objectives:

TIP

Ask yourself this question about each Must: "Would I accept something slightly more or less than outlined in the objective?" If the answer is "yes," then the objective is a Want, not a Must.

- Minimizes cost per participant (Want, 5).
- Offers the most on-site dining options (Want, 7).
- Has a strong reputation for service (as measured by annual hospitality industry customer satisfaction survey) (Want, 10).
- Maximizes seating in the main conference room (Want, 9).
- Has at least 200 rooms available next February 14 to 18 (Must).

Your decision should have at least one objective that is rated a "10" so that you can compare the other objectives to it. You can also have more than one 10-rated Want. Example 6.3 lists, classifies, and weighs objectives for selecting a resource to lead work package 12.1 Technical Manuals Produced.

The final piece of Decision Analysis deals with *alternatives*, and how well the alternatives perform against the objectives. Alternatives

Example 6.3   Decision Analysis—Objectives

Decision Statement

Select a resource to lead Work Package 12.1 Technical Manuals Produced.

Objectives	Classification
Has content expertise (certification in subject area)	Must
Costs no more than $60/hour	Must
Has time to manage the work (unallocated in master schedule)	Want
Understands the publishing process (interaction with the process)	Want
Has managed similar project work before (number of times)	Want
Willing to take ownership (exhibited similar behavior on other projects)	Want
Has experience writing technical manuals (years of experience)	Want
Will work well with the team (has established a relationship)	Want
Can provide thought leadership to the team (ability to influence the direction of the work based on expertise and communication skills)	Want
Minimizes cost to the project	Want

Want Objectives	Weight
Has time to manage the work	10
Has experience writing technical manuals	9
Willing to take ownership	8
Can provide thought leadership to the team	7
Will work well with the team	6
Has managed similar project work before	3
Understands the publishing process	5
Minimizes cost of the project	4

TIP

You can also use Decision Analysis to recommend a choice to stakeholders or customers. To do this, complete the Decision Analysis process and record the results in report form. The report should contain your preferred choice as well as the main reasons you selected it and any risks associated with it.

are possible choices that you consider for your decision. First, record all the alternatives that you and others propose. Then, take each one through your Must objectives. If the alternative doesn't meet the Must set limit, then discard it. For example, if you set a Must as "Provides a two-year warranty at no additional cost," and two of your alternatives do not, eliminate these two from consideration. (As you can see, it's very important that each Must objective is truly mandatory—not just an important Want.)

After testing the alternatives against the Must objectives, compare them against the Wants. Which alternative best satisfies this objective? How well do the others satisfy this objective? Now, you'll use a 10 to 0 scale, and it will be used to score the alternatives. The alternative that best meets the objective receives a "10." The rest receive a score based on how well they meet the objective compared to the "10." More than one alternative can merit a "10" if each alternative satisfies the objective equally well. Repeat this process for each objective.

In Example 6.4, the alternatives have been tested and compared. The numbers you see in the alternative cells represent the score, as well as the weight multiplied by the score. For example, Product Development Associate scores a "10" for "Has time to manage the work." The "10" is then multiplied by the weight ("10") to get "100." This is represented by "10/100."

Add the multiplied scores for each alternative to get a total score. For example, the total score for the Product Development Associate would be 440 (100 + 63 + 80 + 35 + 60 + 30 + 40 + 32 = 440).

The alternative that scores highest may be your best choice. However, you first must assess risks and potentially adverse consequences. Ask, "If we choose this alternative, what could go wrong?" This will give you a list of risks. For each risk, ask, "If this risk happens (probability), what will be the consequences (seriousness)?" Then rate the probability and the seriousness of each risk using a High-Medium-Low scale.

Example 6.4 Decision Analysis—Alternatives

Objectives	Weight	Product Development Associate	Training Senior Associate	Publishing Editor	Contract Resource
Cost no more than $60/hour	Must	$40/hour	$55/hour	$40/hour	$35/hour
Has content experience	Must	Is certified in subject area	Newly certified in subject area	Is unfamiliar with subject matter	Is certified in subject area
Has time to manage the work	10	Is currently available 10/100	Schedule is open currently 10/100		Is currently available 10/100
Has experience writing technical manuals	9	Has 6 years' experience 7/63	Has 3 years' experience 4/36		Has 10 years' experience 10/90
Willing to take ownership	8	Has proven track record (8 years with company) 10/80	Fairly new to the company (one year only) 6/48		Has indicated willingness to make "top priority" 8/64
Can provide thought leadership to the team	7	Has not yet demonstrated this ability, but has knowledge and experience in subject area 5/35	Does not have enough experience in subject area 2/14		Background and experience in subject area will be an asset 10/70

(continued)

Example 6.4 Continued

Objectives	Weight	Product Development Associate	Training Senior Associate	Publishing Editor	Contract Resource
Will work well with the team	6	Has established relationship with entire team 10/60	Has worked with some team members 7/42		Will be new to the team 3/18
Has managed similar project work before	3	Has done so 5 times previously 10/30	Has never done so before, but has project management experience 5/15		Has done so 4–5 times previously 10/30
Understands the publishing process	5	Understands the business well (8 years' interaction) 8/40	Has some knowledge of the business (3 years' interaction) 3/15		Has spent many years in the business (10 years' interaction) 10/50
Minimize cost to the project	4	$40/hour 8/32	$55/hour 5/20		$35/hour 10/40
TOTAL		440	290		462

188

Are you willing to handle the risks to get the benefits of this alternative? If your answer is no, consider the next alternative. Now that you've examined both the results and the risks, make your decision.

Look at the alternatives in Example 6.4 (pp. 187–188). "Contract resource" scored the highest at 462, but before making a selection the decision makers viewed some of the risks and adverse consequences for the highest performers.

The decision makers examined the risks and adverse consequences associated with selecting the product development associate and the contract resource (see Example 6.5). After

PITFALL

Don't eliminate a high-scoring alternative simply because it contains significant risks and adverse consequences. First determine whether you can take action to minimize the risks and handle the adverse consequences if they do occur. Then decide if you need to consider the next-highest-scoring alternative.

Example 6.5   Decision Analysis—Risks

Risks and Adverse Consequences

Alternative: Product Development Associate

Risk	Probability	Adverse Consequence	Seriousness
If she continues to be involved in major projects for other clients,	M	Then conflicting interests may prevent her from devoting sufficient time to leading this work package.	H
If assigned responsibility for other work packages on this project,	L	Then she may be distracted from leading this work package.	M

Alternative: Contract Resource

Risk	Probability	Adverse Consequence	Seriousness
If he finds other more attractive (higher-paying, longer-term) contract work,	H	Then he may not want to or be able to play the leadership role as expected.	H
If the schedule slips and we are unable to provide him with work at the agreed-upon time,	L	Then he may not be available when the work has to be done.	H

determining they would be able to manage the risks, they selected the product development associate to lead the work package.

Record the actions you need to take to implement the decision. Make sure you include any actions you need to take to prevent or prepare for the risks and adverse consequences.

PROBLEM ANALYSIS

Problem Analysis is a step-by-step process that helps you find the cause of a problem. However, Problem Analysis should only be applied if your concern meets the following qualifications:

- It represents a deviation between what should be happening and what is actually happening. For example, a work package is delayed because a prototype failed in testing.
- You don't know the cause of the failure. If you already know the true cause, you should decide what action to take to fix it.
- You need to know what caused it to fail in order to take the most appropriate action.

Where to Use It

If your concern qualifies, Problem Analysis will provide a means for revealing the true cause of problems in Planning and Implementation. Here are a few areas where Problem Analysis can be applied:

- Finding the true cause of problems that occurred with similar projects in the past (to better define and plan the current project).
- Finding the true cause of something that goes wrong with your plan during implementation. This can include delays, inaccurate budget estimates, and not-as-expected output.
- Resolving the people problems that occur during a project.

Example 6.6   Problem Specification Questions

Dimension	Is Question	Is Not Question
What	What specific (object) has the (deviation)?	What could have the (deviation), but doesn't?
	What specific (deviation) does the (object) have?	What deviations could the (object) have, but doesn't?
Where	Where is the (object) when it has the (deviation)?	Where could it have been when it had the (deviation), but wasn't?
	Where on the (object) is the (deviation)?	Where could the (deviation) be on the object, but isn't?
When	When was the first time the (object) was observed to have the (deviation)?	When could it (object) have been observed first with the (deviation), but wasn't?
	When since the first time has the (object) been observed with the (deviation)?	When since the first time could the (object) have been observed with the (deviation), but wasn't?
	When in the object's life cycle did the problem first occur?	When in the object's life cycle could the problem have occurred first, but didn't?
Extent	How many (objects) have the (deviation)?	How many (objects) could have the (deviation), but don't?
	How many (deviations) are on each (object)?	How many (deviations) could be on each (object), but aren't?
	What's the size of a single (deviation)?	What could the size of a single (deviation) be, but isn't?
	What is the trend in the object and/or deviation (increasing, decreasing, or staying the same)?	What could the trend be, but isn't?

Time and budget pressures can cause project managers to jump into immediate action when something goes wrong. However, stepping back and doing a Problem Analysis can save you from wasting time and money fixing the wrong cause.

Steps in the Process

The first step is to write a *problem statement.* A problem statement contains the object that has the problem and the deviation that it has. The deviation is the gap between what should be happening and what is actually happening. Here are some examples of problem statements:

- Work stations arrived late
- Metal cabinets are getting dented during installation
- Dry-skin medication produces bumps on test subjects

The next step asks you to answer a series of questions that describes the problem in four dimensions—What, Where, When, and Extent. This process is called developing a *problem specification.* You'll need to ask the questions in two ways—you'll ask what the problem *Is* and what it *Is Not.*

TIP

If you still need help identifying possible causes, examine each Is/Is Not pair and ask, "What is different, special, odd, or unusual about the (Is information) as compared to the (Is Not information)?" This will produce a list of distinctions that can also provide you with possible causes.

Although it might seem to be a waste of time at first, answering both questions will narrow the problem further. Often, as you'll read later, it's in the comparison between the two answers that you'll find cause. The problem specification questions are listed in Example 6.6 on page 191. In Example 6.7 you will find a completed problem specification for the problem statement "Workstations arrived late."

After assembling the answers to these specification questions, you might have some new ideas about what caused the problem. If no new ideas are immediately forthcoming, hypothesize about what could have caused this problem using your knowledge and experi-

Example 6.7   Problem Analysis—Statement and Specification Problem Specification Questions

Dimension	Is Question	Is Not Question
What	Workstation desks	Workstation returns, lateral file cabinets, hutches
	Arrived late	Missing, arrived damaged, wrong workstations
Where	Vendor's warehouse	Vendor's shipping dock
	Not applicable	Not applicable
When	12 August	Before or after
	Still had not arrived between 12 August and 20 August	Could have arrived between 12 August and 19 August
	Single incident—no pattern	Could have arrived after 20 August
	During preparation for shipping by vendor	During submission of purchase order
		During purchase order processing
Extent	All workstation desks	None, one or two
	7 days late	More or less than 7 days
	Not applicable	Not applicable
	Occurred once	Less or more

ence with similar problems. Record the possible causes you identified and then determine which one best fits the problem description by asking, "If (the cause) is the true cause, how does it explain both the (Is) and the (Is Not)?" The cause that has the least and/or most reasonable assumptions is likely your most probable cause. Example 6.8 illustrates how to identify and evaluate possible causes for the problem statement, "Workstations arrived late."

The final step in Problem Analysis is to confirm that the most probable cause is actually the

TIP

If you're still searching for causes, examine the list of distinctions and ask, "What has changed in, on, around, or about each distinction?" These changes can help suggest causes.

Example 6.8   Problem Analysis—Most Probable Cause

Identify Possible Causes	Evaluate Possible Causes	
	Does not explain...	Explains only if...
Delay during shipping caused late arrival.	Why only the desks were delayed and not the returns?	Desks were separated from the returns during shipping. Desks and returns were shipped out separately.
Vendor's new inventory system delays arrival.	Why only the desks were delayed and not the returns?	Desks inventoried incorrectly.
Purchase order delayed.	Why only the desks were delayed not the returns?	Separate purchase orders were processed for the desks and returns. Decision to buy desk and returns was made at different times. Purchase orders for desks were submitted later than purchase orders for returns.
New purchasing procedures were followed.	Why only the desks were delayed not the returns?	New procedures were followed for the desks and not the returns.
New shipping supervisor intercepted order and delayed shipment of desks.	Why only the desks were delayed and not the returns?	Desks were specifically targeted for delay due to lack of funding.

Determine the Most Probable Cause	Confirm True Cause
Purchase order delayed.	Ask Purchasing whether separate orders were placed for each item (workstation desks, workstation returns, cabinets, hutches) and when they were sent out. Review when the decision to buy the desks and returns was made and communicated to Purchasing. Ask vendor whether separate purchase orders were received for each item and when they were received.

true cause. Do this by testing the most probable cause by gathering facts to confirm it or by watching the problem as it happens. Then assign actions to fix the problem.

Problem Analysis may seem complex at first, but it doesn't have to be. Sometimes, just asking the problem specification questions can help you and others solve the problem.

DECISION-MAKING AND PROBLEM-SOLVING SUMMARY

The processes discussed in this chapter are not a new way of thinking. Situation Appraisal, Decision Analysis, and Problem Analysis simply take the commonsense ideas you may have always used and arrange them in a logical framework. Because they are systematic, thorough approaches to dealing with concerns, they will help you gather and organize information effectively. They will guide you through unfamiliar situations by helping you draw on your experience and judgment. In short, they will help you and your project team deal in a rational manner with the challenges that projects throw your way.

chapter
7

---

installing project management within an organization

ENSURING SYSTEMATIC USE OF PROJECT MANAGEMENT

What distinguishes organizations that have learned the art and discipline of flawless project management and execution? In working with organizations both large and small, in the public and private sector, in the United States and offshore, in manufacturing sites and corporate headquarters, Kepner-Tregoe has found that there are seven conditions that are essential for project success. These seven conditions do not rise to the level of rocket science, but putting them in place can be difficult, especially in the absence of a disciplined approach. Perform poorly against even one of these conditions, and you put your projects in significant jeopardy.

Seven Basic Conditions for Success

1. *Make a Compelling Business Case for Project Management.* All too often, project teams are asked to carry out their work in a vacuum. They are told what must be done, but not why. Not knowing how their efforts will help achieve the organization's strategic goals or what impact they will have on the bottom line typically breeds the "this-too-shall-pass" syndrome. Not surprisingly, many teams lack the motivation to stick with it, losing oomph long before the project is completed.

To convert intent into the will to win, project leaders and their managers need to communicate clearly to each team member, at the beginning of every new project, the value the project is expected to add to the organization. How will the successful completion of the project directly advance strategic and operational goals? Will market share, margins, and/or the size of the market be increased? Will time and the cost of doing business be decreased? Will paperwork be reduced, red tape slashed, or internal communication made easier? The team also needs to be made aware from the outset of the measures and standards that will be used to judge success, not only at the project's completion, but throughout the project management process.

Once the team understands the value of the project, team members must be sold on the value of the project management process. In other words, they need to know the answer to the time-honored question: What's in it for me? How will following this process make my job easier and add value to it?

Here is one way to demonstrate convincingly the importance of following a common, codified process: Compare the results of past projects—those where the process was followed and those where teams "freelanced"—and then go public with the findings. This should be relatively easy to do, given the project management requirement for documentation. It becomes easy to see—and share—the advantages: the deadlines met, the time and money saved, the ending of turf wars, and the elimination of frustrating bottlenecks.

2. *Make Project Management Practical, Relevant, and Beneficial from Day One.* Project management is often associated with technical tools and software. The vaunted Project Management Body of Knowledge® (PMBOK) contains a wealth of literature and training material, dealing with every aspect of project management: from scope control to financial management, from estimating to team building, from communication to contracting, and more. These materials contain many of the lessons learned by project teams over the past few decades.

Unfortunately, much of the existing material is far too technical for the novice project manager and team. To many, following each and every step in the process seems tedious, and the benefits don't appear to justify the investment of time and energy. And, as good as the training materials may be, learning the concepts from a book or in a classroom doesn't guarantee that people will be motivated or able to use them on the job.

Effective project management tools are *not* a replacement for sound judgment by project managers. A key role of the project manager is guiding the use of the concepts so they help rather than hinder the team's progress. Before getting down to work, each member of the project team needs to agree that the process they will be following is realistic and practical. In particular, they need to know the *intent* of the concepts and tools well enough to know *how much* of each to apply.

3. *Make Project Management an Adventure in Learning by Doing.* Some graduates of project management training embrace—even zealously adopt—sound project management methods on their own. But don't count on it. By the time learners return to work, even a minor misunderstanding of the process or the rush of everyday business may cause them to revert to the tried and true.

This puts a premium on building bridges to on-the-job use. We recommend providing learners with venues for applying their newly acquired skills and, just as importantly, supporting them with expert coaching and feedback delivered in real time and at the moment of application truth. This combination will help internalize the learning and drive continued use.

4. *Make Systems and Procedures Project Management Friendly.* Ideally, the process for conceptualizing, approving, initiating, planning, implementing, and closing projects is documented and visible. In addition, it is supported by procedures, forms, workflows, and organizational structure that remove all ambiguity about how project work gets done. And information systems and reporting compare actual project performance to expectations.

Communicating the rationale behind project definition, planning, and implementation is fundamental to the successful use of project management. Explaining the "why" behind each step, along with the rationale for supporting systems and procedures—and then testing understanding—is key to project management success.

5. *Make Project Management a Win for Both Project Team Members and Those Who Manage Them.* People tend to follow the path of least resistance. For a graduate of project management training to actually apply what he or she has learned, using the concepts must not add more work or consume more time than the person's previous approach. Unless the process is perceived as an improvement over previous work methods, people will soon revert to their old, comfortable ways.

People also need positive reinforcement. The organization needs to offer rewards and recognition—financial or otherwise—for the use of project management concepts. People should be rewarded both for their contribution to project outcomes and for *how* they contributed. Those to whom project managers report need to be rewarded for the coaching, support, and oversight that they provide; they need to be held accountable and rewarded for the success of their project managers.

6. *Make Project Management a Continuous Learning Experience.* Projects are incubators for the development of future leaders. Experience on a project team often tests a variety of skills and behaviors, from the ability to work gracefully under pressure and manage conflict to the ability to deliver results on time and within budget. Projects also allow an organization to gradually up the performance ante for high-potential employees, testing their mettle against projects of increasing complexity and risk.

But project experience per se does not build capabilities. After all, merely repeating the same experience time and again leaves you with just one experience! One way to avoid the stunted-development trap is to practice destructive questioning. Do this by ending every project with a tough-minded self-appraisal: What was done well? What was done poorly? What are the lessons to be learned? What strengths and weaknesses can be identified? How can the strengths be exploited and the weaknesses corrected? What should we do differently next time around? The answers may lead to targeting a specific project opportunity; reveal a mentoring, coaching, or training need; or indicate a need to shift responsibilities on future projects.

Whatever the answers, the point is clear. Every project should be a platform for learning and growth.

7. *Make Success Public.* Continued success requires going back often to the reasons the organization felt a need to improve its project management practices. How are projects helping meet the need? What standards are still not being met? How has the need changed? How can the current approach be improved?

Making the answers to these questions visible and communicating them widely makes it clear that the organization is serious about project management and provides reinforcement for use of the concepts. It also helps sway the fence sitters who have been resistant to change. The ultimate message is broadcast clearly: "The way things get done around here has changed forever."

INSTALLING PROJECT MANAGEMENT

Installation is one of those words that is subject to a variety of interpretations. Kepner-Tregoe and its clients surely know what installation is not, especially as the term relates to project management. It is not a big-bang change, the type usually accompanied by wall posters, rah-rahs, and an organization-wide baptism in skills training. True, it is necessary to develop skills and inform people about new practices, but bringing about lasting change requires looking at the organization holistically.

Organizations are complex entities that operate smoothly only when all their elements work together to produce results. In order to achieve the seven conditions for project success, senior management needs to ensure that each of the following elements is aligned and integrated into a coherent framework for project management:

Strategy

An organization's strategy should provide the boundaries for projects; goals and results must flow from an organization's future direction. Before deciding to embark on a new project, and when communicating the goals of that project to the project team, senior management must provide clear answers to the following questions: What are the organization's products and services? Who are its customers and markets? What is its competitive advantage? How will this particular project support the achievement of its strategy?

The best project management organizations have a clear, well-communicated strategy and know how each project supports it. Installing effective project management includes putting in place a mechanism to evaluate every project for its fit with the strategy prior to implementation. This needs to occur very early in the game, during project definition, if at all possible.

In most organizations, responsibility for this strategic evaluation, or screening, lies with the senior management team: the CEO and his or her direct reports, or an executive committee made up of several top managers. As each proposed project is reviewed, this group asks questions such as: How does this project support our future thrust for business development? How does it fit into our current and future scope of products and markets? How is it related to our key capability requirements, our financial and growth expectations, and our cost constrictions? If the answers to these questions indicate that a project is not a good strategic fit, this needs to be communicated to the project's supporters before any more resources are expended.

In some organizations, the Project Management Office is charged with ruling on the strategic fit of projects. This is only possible when the company's strategy has been carefully formulated and clearly communicated from the top down, so that the Project Management Office can answer the previous questions. And, in cases where it is unclear whether or not a project is aligned with the organization's strategic goals, the Project Management Office needs to check with senior management before approving it.

Even if the unit in which the project is being undertaken is part of a larger organization and its customers internal, it is essential to know how it adds value to the overall business strategy and how the project advances the value equation.

Goals

Effective project organizations know which operational goals make a difference and then install methods for keeping these visible to all. At the beginning of a project, senior management needs to agree on, and communicate to the project team, answers to these questions: What are the organization's long- and short-term operational plans and budgets? How does this project fit into or support these? Answers may include targets related to revenue, profit, costs, cash flow, return, brand equity, customer satisfaction and retention, time to market, innovation, efficiency, output, and quality.

Once the project is underway, progress against these goals needs to be evaluated and communicated on an ongoing basis. In some companies, this information is displayed prominently on a "dashboard," keeping critical issues in everyone's sights and ensuring that resources are directed to the areas where they are most needed.

Leadership

By directing the selection and overseeing the management of projects, the top-management team is able to keep a tight rein on the organization's project portfolio. Moving some of this responsibility down in the organization, to a Project Management Office, frees up senior management for more strategic tasks and gives those closest to the action more power.

Each organization must decide for itself how to strike the right balance between control and agility. Whichever method an organization chooses, it will not bring lasting and deep benefits unless it is visible and consistent. The moment projects are initiated outside the system or justified by fuzzy or mysterious criteria, people will drift to informal, random, behind-the-scenes, and/or political methods that undermine the system and the organization's goals.

Business Processes

Within an organization, the systems used to gather, analyze, and disseminate information must support project-based work. This is true whether the projects are external (e.g., a service that a construction or IT company offers to its customers in the marketplace) or internal (e.g., the installation by an organization of new machinery or a new inventory system to improve its own operations). In the first case, tracking the resources spent on any one project is relatively easy, but even then the handoffs between functions need to be clearly delineated and readily adaptable to the uniqueness of any given project.

In the case of internal projects, however, information is not usually dealt with on a project basis. Instead, systems are set up to capture and disseminate information by function: the cost of computer hardware and software, labor, raw materials, travel, and so on. It is up to the project manager to break these functional costs down to ascertain how much has been spent on his or her project. This is easier said than done, however, since functional and project tracking systems are usually out of phase. For example, employees may work on several projects in any one month but then turn in their timesheets to their functional supervisor, not to the project managers. The former must tally up the time spent by each person on each project, then relay it to the respective project managers—creating a time lag that decreases the usefulness of the data to the project managers. In such cases, systems need to be redesigned to ensure that project managers receive relevant data on a timely basis.

Human Capabilities

It's a truism that effective project management requires the right people, with the right skills. Some people are just not suited to the challenges of project management; they do not thrive in the inherently ambiguous and give-and-take environment of projects. Others blossom in it; they love the challenge of working toward a goal and being part of a project team; they love the unique new challenge that each project brings. Such people are motivated by the opportunity to learn. A key skill needed by those who are installing project management is the ability to identify—and to hire and retain—those individuals who are best suited for project work.

But being suited to project management is only part of the equation: As we discussed earlier, the capabilities of team members need to be continuously evaluated. Each project should enhance existing capabilities and provide new development opportunities in areas such as leadership, problem solving and decision making, human performance management, communication, portfolio management, cost accounting, and contracts.

Culture and Performance System

An organization's culture consists of its norms, values, and beliefs. These may be explicitly expressed; often they remain hidden and form part of the implicit context of organization life that can exercise a gravitational pull on decision making. Unless an organization demonstrates visible, unreserved commitment to sound project management practices, the chances are project management will be viewed as just another activity. The successful installation of project management depends on an organization's explicit belief that *how projects are managed is just as important as what they achieve.*

Since managing projects is a team sport, employees in effective organizations not only use the project management concepts themselves but also support others' efforts to do so. Internal project management experts—call them project management black belts—provide both positive feedback for successful use of the concepts and coaching when team members are having difficulty applying their new-found knowledge. Project management becomes "the way we do business around here."

Let's face it, motivation and the rewards that drive it are a private affair. For some, formal, public recognition works best. Others are more financially driven. Still others are "stroke" oriented: Positive feedback delivered personally and privately by supervisors creates an emotional and performance "high." A relatively small number need no external recognition: The satisfaction of applying a new skill is their primary driver. Effective project managers know what motivates each member of the team and reward success accordingly.

Information and Business Systems

Systems and procedures are channels for the repetitive, functional aspects of the business but, at best, do not support project work and, at worst, impede it.

For example, financial systems tend to lend themselves to reporting, say, capital consumption, but may be less effective in capturing the "burn" of projects. Procurement procedures may work well to track and control purchases, but they are less likely to sync with the typical stages of project approval or predict cash flows for project work that has been completed but not yet reported. Time reporting has long been useful in capturing individual activity but not who may have worked on which project—and it may not be timely enough to serve as a useful management tool. Over the past decade, project management software has become a superlative tool for organizing and representing project information, but it has its limitations. For one, it is not a substitute for project management skills and the judgment required to apply them. And project management software is often deployed as an isolated tool, disassociated from the organization's other information systems.

The best way to integrate and align new systems and procedures into the business life of an organization is to make them relevant to the way business is conducted, which means they must prove value added, just as every other project is expected to do. In other words, they must address: What value should this project create? What resources will it require? Who will do what, when? How will risk be managed? How does the project compare to expectations? And what have we learned?

Issue-Resolution Systems

Projects are usually initiated to resolve an issue. Projects produce countless issues to be clarified, decisions to be made, risks to be avoided, and problems to solve. The best project organizations know how to quickly assign ownership of an issue to a project team, have it move smartly to analyze the issue using agreed-on problem-solving, decision-making, or planning methods, and then move to resolution. They avoid the proliferation of "gray beards"—projects that hang around forever and dull an organization's competitive edge.

Since projects are often initiated to meet a one-time need and frequently cut across the organization, existing chain-of-command and escalation processes may not apply to them. It is important, therefore, that the organizational structure, project governance, and/or individual project ground rules be made clear: what the project team is responsible for and authorized to do, how decisions will be made within the team, and what will be the expectations regarding buy-ins and handoffs.

Team Structure

There is no one best way to structure project teams. Installing project management requires matching the team structure to the project and to the other needs of the business.

Several options exist for organizing people for project work. One common approach is *matrixing*, where reporting responsibility is divided between project and functional managers. One caveat: As "slaves to two masters," project resources may develop divided loyalties, and rivalry between the project and functional managers may erupt into open warfare.

Intact project teams that move together from one project to the next are another option. This structure tends to build high-performing teams that greatly leverage lessons learned from previous projects, but it may not be the most efficient deployment of the organization's resources. It may also limit the speed and depth of team members' personal development by limiting the opportunities that they receive.

The central pool is another common approach; here, resources are on call to meet demand. This affords the greatest efficiency, gives the greatest range of development opportunities, and fits well with the use of temporary and contract resources. But it also requires a strong scheduling function, with the authority to stand up to demands for specific resources. Nor does it work well if the bulk of the organization's work consists of nonproject, functional tasks.

Whichever team structure an organization chooses, it is critical that changes be made carefully to avoid disrupting work in progress and to give the people involved time to understand the change and become comfortable with it. Serious consideration and care must also be given to those who might not fit into a new structure.

External Factors

Installing project management implies emphasis on the internal workings of the organization, but external factors are also at play. Certain customers and markets may demand that projects be conducted in a special way. In the case of external projects—those with a mission that takes them beyond organizational boundaries—this may require changes in the way the projects are sold, delivered, or reported on. For internal projects, one of the biggest challenges is gaining and sustaining organizational commitment to the project: competing external customer and market demands have a way of preempting attention and resources.

In today's dog-eat-dog environment, competitive advantage must be extracted from everything an organization touches and does. Remember that superior project management skills and the innovative practices, processes, and products they spawn can be an important competitive differentiator. Top management needs to continually benchmark the organization's skills in this area against those of the competition and make whatever investment it needs to keep pace.

Government regulations must also be factored into the organization's project management process. They may require that work be conducted or documented in a certain way; they may impose procurement and bidding constraints. Laws and regulations may even routinely add work that must be integrated into the scope of your projects.

Vendors and suppliers need to be aligned to support project work. The right materials—whether raw materials arriving at the dock or just-in-time information from external sources—must show up at the moment of need. Contracts and procurement processes need to be aligned with project schedules, and rewards must follow both supplier and buyer performance.

The future, by definition, is indeterminable, which means that no organization possesses all the capabilities it will need to face the challenges that lie ahead. But steps can be taken to prepare for the unpredictable. For example, careful succession planning and continuous training and development of future project managers will ensure that the requisite talent will always be on tap to tackle new projects as they arise. In this, the human resources function plays a key role. As organizations reach out to confront the future, human resource professionals must be acutely aware of the new skills that upcoming projects may require and the new opportunities these present to green the next generation of leaders.

HOW SHOULD YOU INSTALL PROJECT MANAGEMENT IN YOUR ORGANIZATION?

The clients with whom we work typically select one of two methods to install project management in their organization: an organizational, or top-down, focus versus an individual, or bottom-up, approach. In practice, neither method is inherently better than the other, and usually some mix of the two is used.

The *organizational focus* addresses a specific project or project need that top management deems critical to the organization. It could be the need to implement a strategy, speed a product line to market, implement an IT initiative, and the like. With organizationally focused projects, the entire installation effort is geared to addressing priority business concerns.

Not surprisingly, the project teams most closely associated with such projects are targeted for training. Workshops are scheduled and tailored to ensure that the concepts are applied to the projects in a way that will maximize the project team's ability to resolve a business issue. In these situations, transferring project management skills is too important to be delegated. For example, a product development team may be targeted to develop and implement projects that will minimize time to market. Or an engineering and maintenance team may be targeted to reduce the time required to implement a changeover on a production line. Line managers themselves are typically selected to train and lead others in effective project management. They serve as internal experts and coaches to support and extend the use of the concepts. It is during this initial phase that the organization's processes, structures, systems, and procedures are modified as necessary to best support project work.

Moving forward, additional teams are trained to more fully address the concerns, and team members are given opportunities to further develop their capabilities. Throughout, top management receives reports detailing the building of the project portfolio, progress on individual projects, issues that they need to resolve, and progress against organizational goals. In time, a critical mass of people is using the concepts, and the revised infrastructure is providing them the support they need to be successful. At this point, it can be said that project management has truly been installed, or "institutionalized," and the most critical needs of the organization are being addressed directly, as soon as they arise.

The *individual focus* approach is used when top management feels that the organization's project management skills and practices are generally deficient. The aim is to improve individual capabilities throughout the organization, thereby raising performance on all projects, no matter what their priority.

Here, training follows a more traditional skill-transfer path. Workshops are scheduled in which either entire project teams are trained together or individuals work on smaller projects or portions of a project to test their mettle. Coaches and process experts are selected from the general population rather than from the ranks of line management. Both scenarios ensure that learning is related to actual projects, and real-time coaching and feedback are provided. As with the organizational focus, processes, structures, systems, and procedures are modified as the need arises. The aim of both approaches is to reach a critical mass so that project management concepts become a part of the business routine.

A major benefit of this approach is that a great many people can be introduced to the concepts and begin using them quickly. However, the initiative must be carefully introduced to avoid its being viewed as just another "flavor-of-the-month" training experience, completely unrelated to the organization's business goals. To prevent this from happening, top management needs to communicate the connection between improved project management and the achievement of key organizational goals. And, perhaps most importantly, employees need to know that, going forward, the use of project management concepts will be one of the criteria on which their performance will be judged.

Which method works best? We usually recommend the organizational focus because it engages top management and focuses on the issues that are most critical to the organization's success. But, as we stress to clients, for this approach to work, *management must be truly committed.* Lip service here kills installation.

A FINAL WORD ON PROJECT MANAGEMENT

Project management is not so much about controlling activity, managing time, and controlling costs; it is more about sharpening and harnessing the thinking of everyone serving on a project team and directing the organization's capabilities toward achieving results.

This is accomplished by giving people the conceptual tools and process to think about, control, and execute project work. It includes a method for gathering, organizing, analyzing, and talking about project information.

Such information is framed within the context of an organization's strategic goals, the larger project objectives, and the expertise for doing the work. Such project information is also parsed into small, meaningful pieces that direct the work of the project.

Organizations that provide the framework and skills for project-based work put real power in the hands of their employees, transforming a new, more disciplined approach to managing projects in a way that outperforms competitors.

Project management requires deliberate planning and action to create the conditions for success and put in place the strategy, leadership, goals, process, skills, systems, issue resolution, and structure to direct and exploit the dynamic nature of project work. The work is hard, but the rewards are great. If work today is done through projects, as is surely the case, then working smarter on projects will undoubtedly enable an organization to meet, head-on, whatever challenges may come its way.

Index